THIS IS ME (NOT REALLY)

AAROHI SHARMA

ISBN 979-888555066-6

for the ones who've dared to love, and the ones who've dared to leave

Contents

Foreword xi

Preface xiii

Acknowledgements xv

Prologue xvii

  1. Me 1

  2. Chapter 2 5

Epilogue 103

Thank you Mamma, Papa and Anna <3

vii

CREATED AT:

Vectors Publication

TURNING A PAGE IN YOUR LIFE

Foreword

A foreword is a piece of writing that serves to introduce the reader to the author and the book, usually written by someone who is not the author.

When I was asked to write this, I literally had no idea what a foreword even meant. Google says a foreword has to be about the book and has to be to the point. I tried summarizing the book and being to the point but I don't think it's physically possible.

This book is random, and honestly I think that's what I love most about it. It has every single aspect of the daily life of any person. It doesn't have a perfect storyline but while reading it you can feel the continuation. It has the random thoughts you have in the middle of a day, the rants and venting sessions, a lot of puns (because they are very necessary), the whole speech you have ready in your mind for when you find someone who loves a particular show as much as you do, and literally a bit of everything.

The reason I was able to read it in one go was because I could understand what was happening, I could relate to it and feel what I was reading. I think it's a great book because there is no dramatical fantasy (as much as I love those too), but it's just honest.

I've known Rohi for quite some time and I felt like I knew a huge part of her before I read the book. But that did not really help as much as I thought it would. Reading the book made me get to know her more in a way I didn't think it would, in a different perspective. Even if you are a complete stranger to her, you might just seem to get to know her by reading the book.

In all, I love the book because it is random and it is relatable and it is real and it is true.

- Tashvi Patravali

Preface

I had started writing this when I was not in the best head-space mentally. As the months passed by I started to feel better and looking back it's expressing all of it here that has helped the most. I really hope this helps anyone reading even a little..to hear that yes it does get better and I'm glad I can smile back at *most* of the things that made me mad while they were happening. It would make me really really happy if everyone who reads this book relates to what I've written even if it's just on a small level. And I hope this is as fun to read as I found it to write.

Happy Reading!

Acknowledgements

For being as excited as me and supporting me all the way I would like to thank my all time favourites- Richa, Dia, Sanjana Shastry, Chirag, Sanjana Kaneria and Nia.

Thank you Anand for guiding me at every step of the way and making the publishing of this book such a fun experience.

Thank you for designing the cover and writing the foreword, Tashvi. You've truly hyped me up since the very beginning.

Special mention to Dia for the "about the author" and helping with the dedication <3

My dear friends, Vriti, Saima, Araana and all of the PIRATES

And my entire family for being so supportive of me and just for everything

Lastly, I want to thank someone who was my best friend not too long ago and got me into writing, to begin with. The one who I think of when I listen to "Mann Bharryaa"

This ones for every person and place that has affected who I am today in the smallest of ways. The events and circumstances that truly made this book possible.

Prologue

At the most random moments, I will be like wow I'd be a cool main character. Then I'll dramatically change the position I'm sitting and behave as someone is recording me. So, I thought why not change my dream into a reality.

Here goes.

As of May 1st, 2021 I'm a 15year old, in 10th standard. I have not had any nail-biting adventures and I'm not that popular girl at school. Still, I like to think I lead a pretty interesting life. In some ways, I'm that average stereotypical teen but in other ways, I don't even know what a "stereotypical teen" is exactly

so you tell me ;)

1

me

I was born in the summer of 2006 and my parents named me Maghna, after the river Ganga. Living in South India, I never was very fond of my name. It was just so different from the names of all my classmates, and it was mispronounced by most of the new people I met. It does not help my case that my name sounds like Meghna, which is a popular name here. When I introduce myself saying "hi my name is Maghna." People often ask me, do you mean Meghna? I always thought that a person's name had little to no connection with their actual personality. I mean, especially when you are just a baby no one knows anything about your personality. As both my father and mother are pretty religious, we visit at least one famous temple outside Karnataka every year. And this year we went to Haridwar. Yes, the gateway of Gods. Ironically, one of the main four homes of the river Ganga. If you have not figured it out already, I'm a writer, and I do enjoy writing poems too. Like a lot. Not to brag but in less than 6 months I've grown a lot through these poems and I am proud of myself for discovering this side of me. Looking back, the first poem I ever wrote, was on Ganga. I mean I know it sounds very stereotypical but at that moment I didn't even realize it. It was for this school project. In a way, I would not have found my love for writing poems if it were not for this, so I owe it to Ganga na?

"Look at her,
As she moves on, gracefully
She stops for none
For she is absolute
Oh! The festivity
The heart beats on with every clash
Lamps are lit and souls enlightened
She is compelling,
For she is Ganga"

Hundreds of thousands of people come and tell her their biggest secrets, their hopes, their fears, and trust her to make everything better. She's a healer.

Without even realizing it I found motivation and comfort in the flowing water, which in my case is a little like self-love.

You know how you listen to this one song every day and not many other people know that song, they've heard it but don't connect to it anything as you do. It's not exactly popular but just known. To them that song doesn't make a difference in their life, because they can find a new one, but not to you.

I'm that song. I am very loved by the people who care about me but others not so much. You may not always take notice of me when I'm there, but you will surely miss me when I'm gone.

I was bullied and left out quite a bit when I was younger, and I used to read books to distract myself from my miserable school life.

While that sounds like a pretty unhappy childhood, that is the time when I first took interest in reading and writing.

I'd spend hours sitting alone in my school library with the lights switched off and the rhythmic creaking sounds of the fan gave me much comfort between my various adventures with the characters of the books I read.

It has always fascinated me how books can just transport you to another place altogether, change your thoughts, your perspective, make you feel so many emotions towards characters who never existed. It gives me very powerful vibes like that's so cool.

Anyways back to my present life,

While everyone my age is pretty busy following all the recent trends and upgrading their wardrobes every few months, my friends and I do well with just each other's company. In some ways, we are like sophisticated adults, and in others like 10-year-olds. That is quite the combination, but it's just the right amount of mature with that kiddish flare.

With all that being said we all are currently restricted to online video calls and chatting, for the past 15 months. While it is a completely different vibe to have access to the whole world at the single click of the mouse, I'd prefer pre-covid life any day.

These never experienced before times do give loads of inspiration to me as a writer. With every passing day, things change just a little, change ever so slow that it misses the human eye completely.

No one knows how long this pandemic will last, and how many things may remain changed forever. We will all come out as different people than in March of 2020.

I enjoy listening to music and cooking. My favorite pastime would be cooking while listening to music *chefs kiss*

Anyways that is enough about me. Oh, did I mention yet that I have a younger brother? Anyways his name is Trijal.

I was born in Banaras, or Varanasi as it is now called and we moved to Bangalore when I was 2, so I don't really have much memory of my first home there. That being said, I have always felt more attached to that city than Bangalore and I'm just more north-Indian from my heart.

Trijal on the other hand loves Bangalore, which may have something to do with the fact he was born here.

So, I guess that covers most everything about me so we can get into the actual part of it.

2

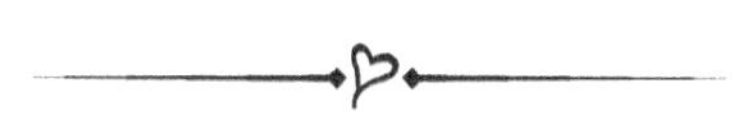

March 12th

Our exams got over today!!! So, 9th grade is officially over. I still can't believe we all managed the full year online. My friends, Navya, Sana, Rashi, and I are meeting tomorrow and I'm very excited. Our results should come in the mail in a few days. I'm, not the best at studies and it doesn't help my case that I'm easily distracted. I worked very hard this year though so let's see.

Trijal has his social exam tomorrow, since he's still in the 5th standard it is online.

"Maghna Didi sun na."

"Kya chahiye Trijal?"

"I don't understand, if all these events happened so long back, not even in India, why are they teaching it to us now?"

I remember asking my teacher a similar question when I was about his age...

"It's so we can learn from the mistakes of others."

I guess that somewhere enables us to appreciate all that we have today because they were not always this way...I thought to myself.

Having a younger brother has always enabled me in appreciating and questioning the small things that usually go unnoticed and only a child may realize.

March 13th

I had a spectacular day! Navya, Sana, Rashi, and I have been friends for over 2 years, but I'd never met Navya and Shashi outside of school. We all came over to Rashi's house and spent the day in her apartment. We played football and ate a lot of junk food. We took loads of photos and for a while, I forgot about how our lives had been disrupted because of the virus. But, when I did remember it again, it worried me that if anything happened to any of us, our families may be affected too some of whom live with their grandparents. I wonder how long it'll take before I can meet anyone without that fear...

March 14th

Our 9th standard results came out today....andd my total average for the year is 71% which sounds pretty average(i mean it is an AVERAGE but you know-) but I'm really proud. I mean I passed Math and all my internals were A's so that's more than enough satisfaction.

Now there are around 2 weeks of holidays before the 10th standard. Yes, I know boards. If it wasn't for Covid we were going to go to Badrinath for the summer. I've gone there before so it's okay that our trip is canceled but we were going to stop at Haridwar during the trip and that's the part that I miss and pretty honestly crave. It does sound odd to crave a place but Man, the vibe there is like no other place. 'Homesick' may be the right term in this context but can you feel homesick for a place that isn't your home? Come to think of it your home isn't always where you're physically present it can be anything, anyone, too...Perhaps Haridwar is my soul home.

For all I know years and years later I may actually live there, physically, and all.

But right now, there's a more important matter in our hands. 15 days at home. What am I gonna doo. I've watched practically all the Hindi movies and most of the English movies of my taste so maybe I should watch some older movies from before I was born that aren't my taste? My thing with shows is a whole other story.

If I find a show I like, I will re-watch it. Many times.

Currently, I've finished F.R.I.E.N.D.S 3 times

The Big Bang Theory also 3 times

The Office 2 times

Young Sheldon 2 times

The Mentalist 1 and a half (currently watching)

Need I go on.

In fact, if I love a specific movie too I re-watch it to the point that even the songs of that movie start to annoy me (sorry 3 Idiots and ZNMD)

While I struggle to learn a single page of Biology for an exam, I can fluently recite the dialogues of something I watch once.

It's weird how our brains also understand what our interests are, enabling us to have the finest memory in the fields of favorite hobbies.

Anyways the problem at hand is WHAT.TO.DO. It's so boring.

March 16th

Imma skip some days in between as nothing too specific is happening during these holidays.

I started using Spotify a LOT more back in January so my total minutes for the end of the year statistics could improve (yes very petty)

But even though my intentions weren't the best I found loads of songs of my taste and now my day isn't complete without music, which can either be just 2 or 3 songs or a good 4-hour jamming session. I am pretty extreme in the things I do if you haven't figured it out yet. My playlists are a healthy mix of Hindi and English. I enjoy romantic songs specifically, but party, sad, lo-fi, mellow, rap I hear it all. I am not the kind of person who listens to those trendy tik-tok songs...in fact, the artists and songs I listen to are not even too well-known. I've spent many a minute thinking how I even discovered these songs in the first place. Beats me.

Trijal and I watched 'Soul' today. It was an amazing movie. It literally has the answer to the question, "What is life?". I am a bigg Disney baby. Coco, Soul, and Ratatouille are my ALL-TIME-FAVOURITES. What I love the most about Disney movies is the fact that even though they are supposedly aimed towards kids, there's always a deep side to things that only older viewers will likely notice. And even though the endings are not always happy as you'd expect them to be, it's still oddly satisfying. The fact that someone can even have an idea for these movies is enough to make me wonder HOW just how. Not only do they have this amazing idea, but they never fail to animate it to perfection.

How can someone animate a body and give it emotions and a personality so beautifully that the viewer actually relates to and gets attached to that character?

For those one and a half-two hours, the people who've made a movie have full control over your thoughts and potentially your full attention. This gives them the ability to change your perspective and outlook about anything literally. That is something that I find to be truly beautiful.

In my opinion, movies should be used as a tool to spread awareness about some topics you may have preconceived notions about or even a topic that is considered taboo. That being said a movie about something as simple as friendship, made from the heart is enough to rekindle someone's faith in humanity.

Damn this got philosophical.

On that note, let's watch the 3rd movie for today, but first, spend around 15minutes looking for something that I may enjoy, get annoyed and end up seeing friends, as usual :)

April 5th

I'm sorry I missed so many days, but honestly, it would have been boring to read about my very monotonous holidays. Anyways, we had our first day of 10th standard today. Apparently, our sections are getting shuffled. My section has been together since the 7th grade and we all have grown to really like each other. So that is sad. Otherwise, the day went pretty well, how you'd expect an online class for 10th to be.

While the scenario outside the house seems to be getting worse by the day I think at least half our year this year too, will be online. Thankfully, all 90 of us are taught together, online so the section thing can be avoided till then I'm assuming. We'll get to know where we've been placed only after a week but hopefully, all of my friends and I haven't been separated. Our school does do a good job of increasing the suspense in such matters. I can only imagine someone saying "Thee shalt not knoweth thy section till a week hast hath passed." Eh well, whatever it takes to feed my anxiety. Seemingly, it'd become hungry with nothing to become anxious over during the holidays, so I don't pin the blame.

I had a video called with Soraya, Vaidehi, and of course Rashi, Navya, and Sana. We played a new game I don't remember its name though. Anyways that was pretty fun. We try and have a call twice every week. We usually watch movies, play games, or just talk.

April 13th

Sorry for not being consistent but who would've thought school would also become monotonous. We have a holiday today. There's no way to say this without sounding I don't know what's the word I'm looking for-

Anyhow many times I randomly feel sad, and it was today that I finally realized that it wasn't my sadness I was feeling. Sounds kind of creepy I know, it did to me too, but I looked into it and you can be heavily impacted by the mood of other people and start feeling what they feel without realizing it, even if these people aren't near you. A more complex form of empathy, I guess.

After I got to know of this, I can differentiate between which feelings are mine and which are simply vibrations of another person. Because everything in this universe is basically a vibration so it's not odd to feel the energies of someone else. Which is quite cool when that person is happy. I mean who doesn't love sharing their happiness. A whole different story for the sad vibes though. The sad feelings make me feel helpless and anxious to help the person, which is not always possible because several times I know who's energies I can feel but this isn't a person I communicate with anymore. The helplessness eats me up and it's hard to snap out of,

MAGHNA, IT'S NOT YOU WHO IS SAD, TO BEGIN WITH.

Why am I an empath...

Ironically, I mostly feel towards people who are no longer interested in maintaining a friendship with me.

"Sweaty palms

Finally gathering up the courage

To write it down

Typing it all in precise detail
Exactly everything she's ever wanted to say
In the words, she wanted to say it
But.
What if they don't reply?
What if they don't understand?
And just like that
Her mind bestrides her heart
As always
At the same time, she can't help but think about what could've been if she hit send
Taping on in great speed, all the words are back
In better choice and framing
Yet,
Something doesn't feel right
Because who expresses their actual emotions on chat after all
She goes back-back-back space
Till just a cursor is left,
Blinking eternally."

Ahh, I couldn't text them to help with this topic of sadness, but I did write this poem for my mental peace. Vented out.

April 29th

Being passionate and ambitious toward even the smallest things does have a lot of positives to it. But in my case at least, there is a lot of negatives too. Major let down. What's hard to believe is that more often than not, I'm let down by my own expectations. Yet, I set them up high for the next time. I'm very hopeful that way.

Anyways I'm writing because we got to know our sections today and my literal biggest fear showed up in the form of an innocent-looking class list.

The dreaded news.

If you're thinking "it can't possibly be that bad", allow me to tell you exactly how bad this is.

Rashi, my best. friend. is in the other section, with Navya and Soraya.

Sana and Vaidehi are in the third section.

Basically, everyone has at least one friend from the group

That's except me obviously.

We've been divided in such a way that of all the original people in my class, only the majority of the boys and 2 other girls are in my new section. None of them are good friends of mine for the record. The boys who could be considered as my friends or at least people I know are fun to be in a class with are all in Rashi's class. My only friend here is Ayaan.

Of all the people from the other sections, no one is my friend either, except Sakshi, who I don't know too well, yet.

I really went from having 18 to 19 friends within my section to 3.

I'm just so epically sad and mellow right now. I mean all this applies only to offline school so I guess I'm good for a couple more months.

The worst thing between all this was seeing that one person who had done nothing but complain about how much he hated the class and all the people in it for 3 years straight, actually being sad at that sight of separation.

"Her smile
Holds a thousand words unsaid
Fighting back tears
She wasn't always this way

And even after everything that has happened
She smiles at every person that comes her way
Sprinkling some positivity into their day seems more important than paying attention to what she feels
Not one person smiles back.
They could have improved her mood...
But she's let down
Consistently and repeatedly
By?
Her own self
HER expectations
"It's fine, I'll be ok"
She consoles herself
Knowing not if that's true"
Wow, that got deep.

On a different note, looking back I feel like I do my best writing when I'm the saddest or angriest...all the words just FLOW out of me if that makes sense¿

Today was a bumpy day but at least I have a break of 15 days from school to get back and face things.

I'm not quite sure what I was expecting with the whole 'section shuffle' but it was ANYTHING but this. Like I said earlier my expectations are already high for even the littlest of things and that is what makes it hurt even more.

2nd May

It is funny how specific sounds, scents, and scenes can transport you to a very specific time in your life. Interestingly, researchers show that in humans there is a unique connectivity between the hippocampus in the brain which plays a major role in learning and memory, and the olfactory system (the sensory system used for smelling). The smell of fresh grass, that song that is played for every occasion at school (no one knows its name), the strong odor of Volini that left some people coughing. Feeling the wind on your cheeks as you pedal faster and faster, till that satisfying and chill downslope automatically transports you to the very bottom. Even the cycle tires make a very distinct downslope sound as you break in order to control your speed. That 2-minute trance after watching a killer action movie and stepping out of a dark movie hall into the light as you say, "ah ok I'm back to reality."

Even though all these things are quite subjective I'm sure you would have heard, smelt, or felt something while reading at least one of them. My wild imagination just played out each of these things sequentially inside my head.

Correct me if I'm wrong, but I'm practically convinced that our brain remembers all these smells and sights that are connected to sad memories far more than the happy ones. Are our senses more heightened when we are sad?

Because the amazing smell of a new book is nowhere as strong as a smell that resembles the aura of a person, someone who you are trying not to think about...

Taste also plays an important role in such scenarios. I know that I've tasted this before, but I can't quite trace it back.

Right! Those hot pakoras in the chilly rain of Badrinath. Looking back, they didn't even taste all that great. It was the weather, the vibe of those mountains, and the company of my extended family that makes that memory soo fond that it's so clear and fresh in my head till today.

The reason for my extreme sentimentality is still the section shuffling. Whatever I do, I'm reminded of that only, again and again. I see pigeons, cherry tomatoes, bhakarvadi's apparently, the song New Divide, a bike, the physics unit "joules", $ this symbol, a stapler, a sippy bottle and last but not least the number 99 in Sanskrit?

As random as the collection of all these things is, I have a very SPECIFIC memory attached to each of these things with different-different people of my *ex*-section.

I tried to wrap my books today, but I kept zoning out while filling the sections. Ugh I kept remembering my section is mine, but all my friends have something else.

"Name

Okay

Class

Yep

Section

All the trauma she just got overcomes flashing back

Why am I in one while you're in another...

Her heart aches 47 times

For she has 47 books to wrap

47 labels to fill

47 times she writers her 'A'

Which was once the same

And so she's reminded forty-seven times that they are no longer in the same class.

Whatever they have today is because of what they don't anymore

Friendships formed and bonds created

For there were only those limited people who became more than enough

Providing support and entertainment at all times

And that's what makes this even harder to accept

There was already a distance being formed before there was separation

And gone,

With no prospect of redemption."

Oh and, I forgot to tell the last time, but Trijal's classes got shuffled too. He is now with all three of his best friends and other close friends.

If there's anything that hurts me more than not getting something I really want, is that if someone else, especially my sibling gets that.

I am sure anyone with siblings will agree.

May 7th/8th

My first all-nighter!!! We had our customary video call for Anvi's birthday at midnight. She and Shashi left within half an hour or so after we played a couple of games. Sakshi, Laya, Trisha, Srishti, Adhya, Preksha, and I stayed till around 4 AM just speaking and playing. We shared some crazy experiences and died laughing mid-yawns. We had a great time. Srishti and Laya stayed on the call till 7 AM. It was soo cool. They both are among my oldest friends, we've been friends since we were 3years old, and we can legit talk forever about anything and everything. It went from very deep conversations to I don't even know what-

In fact, we all go to the same school.

The three of us witnessed the sunrise and it was reallyyy pretty and amazing. I'd only ever been awake till 5 AM or so before, so this was a very new and amazing experience.

By the end of it none of us were even sleepy. So, we just cut the call and went about our day.

I lasted till like 10 AM and slept till 1 PM. Even though that is like 3 hours, I consider that nap length.

I'm done with all the homework for school so that's nice, I guess. I do have to complete my tuition notes, as I had taken a month's break. Laya was kind enough to send me her notes for reference. Dhwani had taken a break with me. We are both back and Algebra it is.

In case I did not mention it yet, Math is my least favorite subject at school. I passionately dislike it. Like all chapters. I have come to peace with it as it's my last year learning Math anyways, yay! (I'm going to drop it as its optional in 11th and 12th grade)

Social Science is my favorite subject. History, Demo politics, and Economics mainly. Geography not so much. And English of course.

I like the law part of democratic politics the most and comparing the different forms of government at present with what they were before. Demo politics and History go hand in hand that way and Economics is a whole another story.

Going ahead I want to pursue Psychology as a subject. Psychology is something that has always amazed me. I may just make a career out of it if I enjoy it in the 2 years that I study it.

Forensic psychology is what interests me the most. *Enter Patrick Jane*

Forensic psychology involves applying psychology to criminal investigation and the law. A forensic psychologist practices psychology as a science within the criminal justice system and civil courts. It involves assessing the psychological factors that might influence a case or behavior and presenting the findings in court.

This perfectly balances two things that interest me the most, law and psychology.

Oh, oh and mango season is officially here. Mangoes aren't exactly my favorite fruit but there's no one more excited than me when it's time to cut the season's first mango.

I will proceed to eat 2 mangos every day for 2 weeks straight and then forget about the fruit till the next year. Very odd I know but that's how I am with most things.

I'll move on to lychees, then cherries, and then jackfruit, maybe guava somewhere in the middle. Eventually, sometime in September, I will start awaiting the mangoes again.

I'll then settle for a humble salted cucumber.

"Seh lenge thoda" *I truly hope someone gets this reference*

-control uday. control-

Damn this conversation got fruity.

May 17th

I watched "Rang De Basanti" today. It wasn't that great a movie or at least I didn't like it too much. But I loved a few aspects of it. I especially loved these lyrics from the song "Roobaroo".

I loved all the different meanings of fire and everything the flame represented. It was truly inspiring. So, this is what I wrote.

The Dazzling Dazzler

"There's a flame

Blazing from within

All shades of orange

Prominently pretty

But oh so dangerous

Always made to hide

Her truthful power

Shh no one can know

Once it gets out

It's hard to control

Impossible almost

It wasn't meant to cause destruction anyway
Why
Why can't anyone see that
She's so dainty and calm
Innocent, if you allow her
It's impossible to stop her once you anger her
But, if you let her be
See her, for her...
Why couldn't anyone see her true beauty?
Just know that
Now that she's ablaze
She's unstoppable"
May 27th

School was supposed to start in a few days but turns out it's been postponed. To make matters worse, and I mean W.O.R.S.E we have been shuffled again and now these sections will be followed online.

Greatest fear becoming true

It's like I keep fearing bigger stuff and it just presents itself in front of me :')

As it turns out, even a second time almost none of my friends are in my section. To make matters worse, they're all together and I'm the only one from the group in another section :(

Soraya, Vaidehi, Rashi, Navya, Sana from my original section and, Srishti, Trisha and Laya are in the other class, ALL TOGETHER.

With me, there's, Sakshi, Preksha, Adhya, and Anvi. Obviously, I'm damn grateful to have a few of my friends in the section but I'm not going to lie, it going to be weird without the people I've been with for 3 entire years. Only about 5 people of that section are in my current class.

The silver lining in this stormy cloud would be that I have Hindi class with the people of my previous section (we had been divided based on our 2ndlanguage in 7th grade)

So, if that's some compensation.

This was my last chance to be in a classroom(ish) environment with some of these people before they changed their schools. This was my last. chance. So, naturally, that upset me a lot and me being me I cried a LOT. I guess I finally figured out the secret to my vibrant and supple skin. TEARS it is.

On a different note, the F.R.I.E.N.D.S reunion aired today! And it was definitely one of the highlights of my entire year. You could say it made my day, week, month, and year :P. Friends is my comfort show. At least one of my comfort shows. Not even exaggerating, I know the show byheart scene-by-scene, that is the kind of concentration I watch it with even after seeing it 3 entire times already. For the 2 hours, while watching the reunion, I forgot everything that I had been worrying me the entire day. The show and all the actors, writers, and everyone involved, are all very powerful that way. Imagine being that impactful, in a good way obviously. Helping thousands and thousands of people get out of their hard times and bringing a smile to someone's face, who had likely given up.

So, my day did end well.

It fantasizes me how my days always end on a balanced note if not a good one. The ways of the Universe never fail to amaze me. Come to think of it, even when I am the saddest, I barely go to bed sad. There is ALWAYS that little something that switches me over from bleh to meh. Maybe, just maybe there IS always something to be happy about in that way, we should just have the drive to look for it.

We often miss out on amazing moments only because we don't have the resolution to be "happy". What is happiness anyway? You decide.

If you truly want to be happy you will find that reason each time. The right intention makes all the difference, to me at least.

If you have accepted that YOU are "sad" even the things another person may describe as happy moments will count as negative to you.

The bottom line to me is that thoughts become things, and no one can help you realize that better than yourself.

Speaking of which, without even realizing it, writing all this right now has substantially helped my mood.

June 2nd

Today was surprisingly greattt. Apart from 7 hours online being extremely hectic, I had fun. I got to 'see' all my friends, classmates, and teachers after almost 2 months and while no one was quite as excited as me, I made up for their excitement too. Although I DESPERATELY miss everyone who is in the other section, there is some level of comfort to this class too. The overall environment of my school and all the people is one that feels like home. Anyways the shuffle wasn't in my hands so I guess I've decided to stop feeling bad for myself and just focus on how I can concentrate more on the people I do have and pay attention to the teacher.

There wasn't anything different as such about most of the classes, and naturally, I enjoyed Hindi the most. There's a different vibe to my section and it just feels right. I was just smiling at my screen for like 2 minutes straight, and I can't be more grateful that I get one class every day. I loved how some people matched my energy and smiled right back. Sir was also in a good mood, so the class went smoothly.

Economics was also really great. I especially love my teacher so that makes the subject all the more fun. We did sectors of the Indian society, and as boring as that sounds I enjoyed learning it a lot.

On a totally unrelated note, we had tuition a few hours after school and it got me THAT tired. So, I have no idea how long I can keep that up.

June 4th

It was a slow day, and our computer teacher changed. I like her but I genuinely dislike the subject, or maybe my issue is with JAVA? Either way except that the day was MoNoToNoUs.

Hindi sir was busy today, so our old teacher came to teach Hindi today and that was surprisingly nostalgic and fun. She had been our teacher for 3 years until this year. At that time, I realized that with ma'am and my *ex*CLASSmates this was as comfortable as online class was going to get. That being said, as weird as it sounds...my bond with some of these people surpass any barriers of distance, time, and in this case, language. Because, just seeing their faces is enough to make my day, and me theirs. We started this new chapter in tuition and its more complicated Algebra :')

June 9th

Adhya and I have become much closer in the past few days. Before, it was just for homework and notes and stuff, but I enjoy speaking to her a lot. Even though we've practically been friends for like 2 years it was mostly because of mutual friends, so it feels great that we're coming closer by ourselves. Along with Economics, I enjoyed English as well. I'm so tired after each day and at this point, it almost feels like I'm living the same day every day. I mean it's nice following a routine and all, with lunch at 12:30 but it gets too mentally and physically hectic and it's just been a week!

Season 2 of The Family Man recently came on Prime and I love this Genre. Murder/thriller, sleeper cells, spy-related, you name it.

Anyways I finished 4 episodes today with my parents and yaa it's nice.

Come to think of it, someone I'm not even in touch with anymore had recommended this show to me like 2 years back when season 1 was released. It's funny to think how so many things just CHANGE after time. At the time, I would have never EVER accepted that he and I would'nt be friends anymore. In fact, I'm not sure I still do.

June 12th

I know I'm writing pretty short accounts, but my days aren't going too differently from one to another, so I thought I can at least write something within fewer days.

Anywho, I finished The Family Man...it was pretty amazing. And there's going to be a season 3 so I'm VERY excited about that. And it's a Saturday so I'm free *more like jobless* but it was a nice chill day. Nothing out of the ordinary :)

It's been less than 3 hours since I wrote the above one and now.

OKAY, scratch that. We got shuffled, AGAIN. No kidding. And as luck has it, I'm.in.the.same.class.

We were doing okay with 45 people per class, now it's 30. They added another section...

Rashi, Sana, Soraya, Vaidehi, Srishti, and Trisha are still together but their section changed. Navya is in the other section, with Preksha, Laya, and Sakshi.

Let's just say if there's anything that hurts more than being separated from all your friends once, it's being separated from them thrice.

So, of my very limited friends, 2 people are now in the other section. Luckily Adhya and Anvi are still with me!

June 15th

I.M. S.O. S.I.C.K. O.F. T.H.E. M.O.N.O.T.O.N.Y.

"5 people

10 eyes

10 people

20 eyes

dot dot dot

more and more

every person and each eye's point of focus

unique and unique

lost in their world

those timeless moments

in their own mind

each has their dilemma

and their tale,

unspoken

looking at each other

face to face

but not quite SEEING the next person

even the eyes are starting to mentally ignore those who aren't seemingly important

just staring at their own face until even that feels weird

those mental ignorance's become important only when they're taken away

it was only later, that it was realized that we were constantly looking at a person other

who is not anymore

well, it wouldn't be known this was the case if it wasn't taken away…
oh, there's still some time left
hmmm
staring into space
what seemed like forever
has come to its end
well so that's 40 minutes of a meeting
5 more to go!
7 more tomorrow and then the day after
again and again
forever and ever"
Wow, it feels so good to get that out of my system. So that's me venting about online classes and tuitions and just everything.

It is really starting to get to me. The long hours, almost no company, and my sore back.

I've reached a point in The Mentalist where I now remember everything because I've seen like the last two seasons a year back.

Because of the entire 3 section situation, they have appointed another teacher for history and demo politics to us, and I'm not happy about that, AT ALL.

At least I still have Geography and Economics. Thrice a week. (compared to the 7 classes we had previously) The dates for our first exam have also come, so I'm going to start preparing for that soon too.

July 20th
Well. It's been a hell-of-a-month

I haven't written anything in over a month and I was not quite sure how I wanted to proceed.

If I did.

Allow me to explicate

First of all, I'm so sorry!! I know it's been a month and 5 days since I last wrote and well, truth be told as a reader I REALLY wouldn't care if even 2 months of my characters life were missing from a book, as long as the plot was interesting

But as in this case, I AM the character I should probably ignore my overthinking-self from accounting everything from a reader's POV.

So,

I mentioned earlier school is monotonous.

to lengths.

And my days were not going well enough to write about or even think about. Some aspects that did keep me going were just by-products of my monotony.

That being said, I did journal every single day, as I was afraid.

Afraid if I did not write it all down, I'd just forget it all and there would ACTUALLY be nothing to distinguish this day from the next and the next.

10th grade is already hard enough, and we had our first exams. Which according to me went pretty well. As well as they go.

We didn't get our results yet though.

So, coming back to what I was saying, each day felt the same, in some aspects... if not all. The things I went to for comfort unfortunately either provided me the same level of tediousness or just changed right in front of my eyes.

Two of my closest friends had an argument that affected me in ways I would have never imagined. They said some things they did not mean, and that was it. I've known them for half my life, and I can say sure as anything that THIS CANNOT BE IT. But for the time being this is what both of them want. In a group of 4, when 2 people are no longer friends, there isn't a group anymore either, just a duo of friends who miss the other 2.

At a certain point, I felt like everything and everyone I'd known and gone to for some form of comfort was just being stripped away from me, faster than I could react.

That is why it is so important that I continue writing, right here, right now. I mean this right here, may not be my best work but it's straight from my soul trust me. And if I do not continue now, I don't know if I ever will.

Everything seems to be CHANGING in my said MONOTONOUS life.

And that right there, my greatest fear and tragedy presenting itself, in truth.

Something very worth mentioning here is from personal experience, in this past month I truly realized the importance of the company of the right people. I am truly blessed to be surrounded by my amazing friends and family. Even small things like story replies and short calls with the right people light me up from inside and give me that hope I need if I am having a bad day.

And music really helped me cope. Through this, everything. I cannot get through a day without music. Like right this second too I am listening to something.

Earlier I used to just hear music when I was bored or felt like dancing, but now I want to dig deep into the meaning. Where earlier I used to listen to the beat, I now focus on the tone and lyrics of the artist. And that is one of the purest things my ears have heard, true words, being sung, in a sweet, sweet voice.

And every time there is that one line, that stands out. The thing that I can relate to in my life. The thing that reminds me of a person, who is maybe not in my life anymore. That reminds me so much of certain situations that I think "this is about my life". The thing that transports me to a very specific timeline in my life- my favorite song when I was 7, the song that I danced to every time- before I even learned how to walk, the song that one of my friends introduced me to but is now my jam. I know the lyrics of so many songs that are from movies released way before my birth. Movies I never watched. Songs I have not heard in over 10 years, but I know them. Word to word. I do not know how, but I can sing it out loud because it just relates to me in more ways than I know to explain.

The most beautiful thing among all this is that the artist who wrote all this does not have the faintest idea of what me or the other millions of people listening to their songs are thinking about. 1000's of people listen to a song on the radio, with 999 having completely different thoughts in their mind, some enjoy the beat, some try to understand the lyrics, some relate, some regret, and that 1 person has the radio playing just as a background to some deep thought on a long drive. The artist perhaps sang about a beautiful moment in their life, but their very way of EXPRESSING it, made me think of a moment that resembled and resonated to THAT song in a better way than the situation they sang about, to begin with.

"Each situation, each idea as distinct as the other
And no situation is the same
But it is the same song
The same beat
And the same lyrics
That fills every heart

With hope and nostalgia."

July 21ˢᵗ

There is something about this date that sounds pretty a d
v e n t o r o u s in itself. I don't even know-how. Like imagine
the host of a game show yell "it is the twenty-first of July!". *I
know hosts of shows don't announce dates out of the blue
but it's fun to imagine*

Like I mentioned yesterday, even though my days
weren't going that great, I did write it all down.

So, I thought it would be fun for me to compile that and
add it here *kind of like a very cool reel in which people
merge 3-second snippets of many different days*

YOU ARE ENTERING A VERY CANDID ENVIRONMENT.

I cut my hair short!!, Adhya and I are becoming pretty
close and chat a lot *sometimes during school* and she
has a very cool sense of humor...I'm glad we have come
closer because of the class shuffling, the text of a specific
somebody made me veryyy happy and the *vibes* of the
text showed me they were happy too. I had a couple of
rough days after this trying to help somebody come out of
a bad space but ended up miserable too. Well as long as I
could make a difference in someone else's day.

I started bullet journaling!! *kept that up for 5 days- I
must continue now that exams are over*, I ate some VERY
tasty mangoes- and drank loads of mango shakes, met my
grandparents after 2 months, and started simultaneously
re-re-re watching like 3 shows.

Oh and on.. the 30ᵗʰ of June I believe, my internet
connection was extremely bad during one of my favorite
classes. So, I wrote a poem about it!

Face to face, miles apart

"The favorite corner of my room

The one I share
With you
Looking at each other
There one minute
And off the next
Who knew
921,600 individual pixels
Could make 2 people feel so much
An entire day may just get destroyed because of the bad connection of a minute
But
They're
Help help helpless
This is their only shot
For this is the only way of seeing one another, blurry if not proper but please don't switch it off
What was there
Was never actually
T h e r e
I just sit there sometimes
All alone
And smile
Imaging you ahead
Like a psycho to myself
It's not much, 40 minutes everyday
But I would not miss it for anything in the world
Be it some person spotlighting themself or when the connection is unstable
Even when it gets
Frus frustrating
How much longer till I can see those eyes and touch that face
Well

It seems closer every time I * zoom * in
Machines may take over the planet someday they say
But the day has already come fellow-being
And that
Is the power of the internet
For the control of their relationship
Resides in the hands of the one without a face"

Let that sink in. just kidding

Imma continue my oddly long list

I met Rashi after veryyy long and we had loads of fun *as we always do ;)*

School's timing changed. It starts late and ends earlier now..they just removed all the breaks between our classes. So, school is a bit more hectic now. We had this series of tests in tuition and attending them was quite fun. When I'm writing notes or solving sums of Math there's usually music always playing in the background so that keeps things interesting and me interested. I met Sana and Preksha in the middle too and we had loads of fun as well. And just today I met Dhwani, after almost a year!

Remembering all these moments made me happy in the present, so I will continue to write and always remember the highlights of even my bad days.

main character vibes

Pun intended :))

22nd July

Wow, I just realized I've used the word monotonous in practically every entry in 2 months.

So sorry about that, I mean it just emphasized what I'm trying to say but like-

At this very second, I'm making a disgusted face, because this is the 3rd ad, I've gotten on Spotify in the past 10 minutes.

Bringing down the scale of my randomness, we will mostly get our exam results tomorrow. I'm pretty excited about that- I guess. Did I mention yet why I am writing this book?

For starters

I absolutely love writing- anything, and I feel I have some amazing things to share and offer to anyone willing to read what I write. And when I say anything, I mean that I love writing unnecessarily long texts for the most random things and ranting to my diary. All this is just the surface reason, I mean anyone who knows me well enough would know this.

But there is a deeper reason that I've never said out loud, that means much more to me. The first book (a 20 pager when I was 11 or 12 years old) I wrote was for a birthday gift to Trijal. I've written letters and long accounts about friends and family and even poems about people whom I don't even know.

Till one day, I realized I never really did much, for ME. Everything was in my taste, but it was never about my happiness or what I actually felt.

I mean what have I ever achieved that's truly 100% me?

While we are on personal achievements,

Honestly speaking(writing) I have never won any prizes or medals for anything at school, dance, sports, or even writing. I participate in almost everything, each year. Of course, there is more to achieving things than medals and trophies, but my wins are things I know, in heart or soul. I have nothing to show for it.

So, I decided to write a book. About me. Authentically. I can say for sure I will read it years later and remember a part of me I had forgotten. If anything, this is for me to understand myself better. I want to publish this and have it with me on my Sweet Sixteenth. I've lost count of the number of times I have imagined the feeling I'll have when I hold my book for the first time. Tiny little parts of me tightly wound together on sturdy paper and things that make me, well ME. Holding that close to my heart, I feel proud just thinking about it. An amazing feeling.

Damn, I was so into writing today that I completely forgot to do my Math HW. So I shall write again tomorrow.

25th July

See. This is my issue. When I don't do something for long, I feel guilty and do it with so much hard work and diligence. This phase lasts for only like 3 days.

I had been writing every day without fail like a good child and got lazy now. Anyways today was a Sunday and we will mostly get our exam results tomorrow.

I purposely didn't write on Friday (23rd) but I think it's worth mentioning that Friday, was one of the best days I've had in a while. The odd part of this is that I don't know what exactly made me this happy. Because my day was more or less the same as every, and as a writer, it's the most frustrating feeling. Not knowing how to write down what I'm feeling. This is how I vent. How I analyze my feelings and moods.

And I just

I-

have no words to describe why a specific event made me this happy.

After 2 days of further analysis, I have reached no conclusion

Except for the fact that- I am happy.

I AM HAPPY. Isn't that all that matters?

That's the most important thing.

Why self-sabotage the happiness I CREATED by my mindless worrying.

"Sunshine smiles
And
Puppy eyes
Everything is your disguise
You make me happy
In ways that I've not seen
Why?
Just why
Something stands out each time
Can't I figure this out
w.h.y
Why not,
You know you are happy
Isn't that enough?
Must you know the why
The how and who
Happiness is a *feeling*
Why link it to people and things
When I know I can find it, anytime
Here, right here
Inside of me."

I'm gonna be honest I know this isn't a very great one, but I mean it's cute. I wrote this as a song, singing each line in a nice tune with "why, just why" as the chorus after every few lines ...so in all fairness, I don't know how this would be as a poem.

I wonder who the first person was who felt so warm and fuzzy after a certain incident and was like, this feels great. I've never felt like this before. WAIT, NEW FEELING. Hmm what should this be called

H a p p y

Sound good?

I wish there was a way to know if human beings felt happiness as their first-ever emotion or sadness. And like who was the first to feel...anything?

Going by Disney's logic, it's happiness. Because in Inside Out, Joy came first when Riley was born.

But babies are born crying. I mean I know they cry because they're exposed to an entirely new atmosphere and environment...not like there's a way to know what they are trying to convey exactly.

So, it's a fair debate between the both of them, I guess.

It's so interesting how crying is the only form of communication for babies and as we grow up, we only cry to convey sadness. Now that I think of it, we are BORN crying and learn how to giggle and laugh and smile only as we grow older.

Everything about emotions is very intriguing and thought-provoking, probably why Psychology interests me so much.

Anyways I can go on and on about this but it's getting late so I will end this day's log here.

27th July

What.a.day

We got our results yesterday, and my marks are not how I expected them to be, at all. So, I was pretty mellow yesterday and decided not to write.

I didn't fail or anything, but my results were pretty average itself *and average is not ok for 10th-grade no-no*. Most of my friends and classmates cheated and ended up getting above 35+ on 40. So, I'm practically the only one who got this low. I mean honesty is more important to me, inarguably but it's just not fair! You know. I would rather get 22 by myself than like 36 by copying answers,

But the thing I'm feeling bad about is that I honestly studied and worked hard for this exam.

I feel like whenever one aspect of my life is going well, something has to get spoiled. Like just last Friday I was soo happy because something so amazing happened in an aspect of my life that was not going that great earlier. But now this.

Well, balance is important, I guess.

Oh, and we had to grow this plant for a Geography project, and my plant grew like 2 tiny leaves and died :(

Today was just not my day I believe. I spoke(chatted) to(with) Laya after pretty long though, and we had a great conversation as always.

And Rashi and I speak every day. As always. Nothing new there :)

Dhwani knows the past few days have been rough so she checks in on me almost every day too.

I went down and met Srishti. Anvi and Preksha after pretty long too. Shashi also joined us later.

See, now that I said all these things, I just feel guilty for saying today wasn't my day. because there's nothing to be sad about.

I'm so grateful that I have friends who make me literally forget everything that's making me sad and enjoy the moment.

To be honest, knowing I have friends that can relate to/ share what hurt me, doesn't necessarily reduce the effect of what hurt me or why. That's for me to see and understand by myself perhaps.

I met Srishti's dog after pretty long and we both were so excited to meet each other!! He was shaking his tail so violently and gave me handshakes from both his hands. He is such a sweetheart.

Speaking of dogs, Anvi recently got a pet puppy too! He's still very young so I have not met him yet.

These days, I think, "what difference does it make if I try or not. Because usually, the outcome isn't what I want it to be anyways." I've never dealt well with uncertain situations or just things not going the way I want them to. But never once have I questioned everything, straight out.

I mean actually, what's the point of ANYTHING.

This sentence alone eats up my head because it proves itself to be true little by little every day. Is it crazy to think I may not notice if I missed a day between today and the day after? If I miss a tomorrow, waiting for tomorrow.

Laya pointed out, that this year filled with hardships may just lead to a beautiful destination and make this last year, worth the wait.

But how can I know for sure?

I motivate myself to get through each weekday, somehow. For the sake of the weekend.

But come Saturday...

I do nothing special, or even worth mentioning.

And just like that, it's Monday again.

I mean what even-

It's not even productivity or something. Just in general. Why look forward to things when there's nothing I have to do anyway.

Maybe I should just give this some time, you know.

Time is truly an illusion.

Because as crazy it seems to me, it's been a WEEK since my first entry after the break. 2 months since 10th grade started. One-fourth of my year is over.

As s-l-o-w and repetitive everything is, *I have effectively overused the word monotonous*

Time is still

Fast.

I really hope offline school starts soon. This is a really important year to me. 100% for non-academic reasons.

See the thing is,

No one knows where they're going to go after this. Some may stay in our school and others may change their school.

For all I know, I may go to some other place. Like I KNOW I'm not going to lose anything with the people I'm tight with, and we will maintain that friendship. But what about all the people I'm not too close to? They're still my friends you know.

And even though everyone says "nothing is gonna change and we'll still be friends" that doesn't hold true …

I speak from experience because everyone said everything will be the same even though we're not in the same section anymore. But things did change. We did grow apart.

Anyways I want to get the best of what may be my last year with these people, in an offline environment.

I've seemingly forgotten how that felt. The whole school environment. How was I not bored after entire years…while I'm struggling to get through months of school right now. I REALLY hope by the time you are reading this; everything is back to normal.

As normal as normal can get.

But actually, I want people to read this bit and remember how much they disliked online class and also smile in gratefulness as they are back to offline school.

Future prediction much

I'm going to seem like such an idiot in case some 4th of 5th wave of covid came off and we're still online-

Anyways it's getting late. See you tomorrow!

30th July

Something that makes me very bubbly from within is self-improvement.

From the time I was, say about 3 years old till about 4 months ago, I was afraid of the dark. it scared me not knowing what's out there in the world and that if it's dark there's no telling what can happen and I knew I couldn't protect myself.

I couldn't sleep alone; I had a night light, and I would sprint to my room after I switched off a light on the dreaded days that I woke up to use the washroom between the night. I was just very afraid in general. I would cover my entire body in a blanket and not let a single toe out, afraid someone would grab me. I had two specific soft toys I just couldn't sleep without, and I always slept facing them, to the left. Because the walls and cupboards to my right scared the hell out of me in the dark. I didn't as much as rest my foot on the floor when the light was off, afraid someone will grab me from below my bed *props to the movie Taken for that concept being put in my head, to begin with- the scene when she's kidnapped from under the bed*. All this being said I've never been afraid of horror movies *in fact, I enjoy watching horror movies* and neither do I believe in ghosts.

Nonetheless, as I grew up, I slowly stopped doing all this, one at a time. My nightlight stopped working when I was just about 6, so I just got used to sleeping without it. As for sleeping alone, I slept with my parents when I was scared but my love for my bed forced me to sleep in my room. I started to enjoy my own company. I now subconsciously sleep facing the right most nights and as for my dear soft toys, it's a longer story. I would cradle both of them together in my arms as I held them close to myself, and that would help me sleep. The two of them have gone with me almost everywhere I've been. Be it Singapore, Hyderabad, or

Haridwar, you name it. It still breaks my heart to say that where once I didn't get even an hour of sleep because I didn't have my Doraemon, one fine day I just didn't need him anymore. It wasn't even gradual...one day, I just grew. up. *they are still on my bed with my other stuffed toys when I sleep, I just don't have that need to hold and cradle them to sleep* I used to hold them close to my heart and wish them a goodnight every day. I would tell them about my day and read them stories. Is it fair to them that I grew up just like that? I don't mind my legs not being covered during the night any more and my foot is on the floor, with the light switched off right this second.

Is it weird that part of why I'm not afraid of the dark anymore is because someone who is not physically near me, is making me feel safe? Ironically, they are the ones afraid of the dark and petrified of ghosts.

But all in all, even though everything I mentioned is mostly bittersweet to think about, it's worth mentioning that even though

I miss the girl I was, I'm proud of the lady I'm becoming.

And that's a win for me. Just me.

Wow, I was feeling oddly nostalgic today. It's so weird to think how I'm now old enough to understand the statement "look back". But ya, today was a great day.

31st July

I had a GREAT Saturday. We went out and I had loads of fun spending quality time with my family. I especially enjoyed the drive to and from the destination. I don't think I've mentioned it before but I love drives. Sitting in the front seat, observing the entire world around me, and listening to my favorite music, with my favorite people. Bliss, pure bliss. It sheds light on how little I am in this big, big world. Around so many people and vehicles that I will never see in my life again, helps me gain perspective. Ever since I said nothing is going well per se, it seems like the Universe is making an extra effort to prove my words wrong *touchwood*.

I've just been having such great days off late!! 2 days back I went down in the apartment, and my entire group of friends came. We were ALL together after more than a year. Srishti, Trisha, Laya, Anvi, Shashi, and Preksha. We were down for almost 4 hours, and I truly lost track of time. I remember this line from "Yeh Jawaani Hai Deewani" where Aditi says, "kuch logon ke saath sirf waqt bitane se hi, sabkuch thik ho jata hai". I am blessed to have friends who make me feel each line of that dialogue till my bones. Just spending time with these people makes me feel at peace. The weirdest part is that we didn't plan anything to do, neither did we speak about some deep things. We just sat and walked and spoke in each other's plain company. While we all were sitting, Srishti rested her head on my shoulder and I rested mine on hers, neither of us said anything but we both had missed each other's friendship, so we just sat in silence. At that moment, I just knew everything would be alright.

It didn't matter WHAT that thing was, or WHEN it would fine by, but I just knew.

Wow, it's 00:00 right now.

Must be a sign to stop writing for today, because its technically 1st August, and I don't want to write about a day I've experienced 1 minute of,

so bye~

3rd August

It's a new month! Happy August. My Sunday was extremely eventful and fun! I had a long day from 4 in the morning till 11 at night. I had gone to Mysore with my family.

On the school front, everything is on the same lines still.

AND we got like 5 projects to complete in a month so it's more hectic than ever. I met Anvi's puppy yesterday and he's this tiny and cute creature. I love him already.

And its Srishti's dog's 3rd birthday so naturally I met him today <3

Even though my day went VERY well, this very minute I'm feeling so low and mellow.

And I can't figure out why.

I was just thinking about all my friends and how I'd become their friends in 8th standard and got to be their friend for just a year before we switched to online.

That being said it's so ironic how the past year, was the year I grew closest to them.

Who had thought SEPARATION could bring people CLOSER.

5th August

We started this chapter in Hindi that's all about sadness. Quite literally. And just today, I found myself in a situation where it's not in my hands for me to get out of the situation.

WHICH I didn't get into myself for the record.

So that wasn't fun. As helpless as I was feeling I did realize that it was my actions that led to this *after quite literally freaking out for about 2 hours*.

So, when I finally calmed down, I decided to pen down all my thoughts and

tada! :)

calm IN the storm

"There once lived a happy girl

living her dreams

she led a calm and serene life, peaceful

until

a magical creature made a dramatic entry into her life
turned everything upside down
made her happier than she had ever been,
imagined
or even felt
he gave her reason to life and purpose to fulfill
but like all good things,
he left one day
saying he'd return soon
days and years pass by
she sat all alone in her castle, waiting
sleepless nights with fairy lights
high up on a tower
with her life on hold
her monotonous monotonous life
she wasn't happy anymore
how could she?
But
She was happy before he came into her life
So, she will be after he left
She had to.
Because for whatever reason
He never returned
And that's okay
Because
The fact of the matter is that a perfect person isn't going
to enter your life and correct the things destroyed by
another
In the end,
She saved herself."
I realllyy love this one
And the title means a lot to me because it brings me a
lot of peace knowing that even though everything's not over

and no one knows what's gonna happen, I KNOW I'm going to be okay.

I will make it.

When I feel weak or sad, or both, I write these poems, read them later, and realize just how strong I am.

12th August

This may just be all I write about today, but a few hours back when I was drying clothes at around 11 PM or so... In the otherwise dark sky, I noticed this bright white light and a blinking light. It was an airplane, and it was the perfect distraction from my chore.

For some pre-context

Airplanes are my one fear. *Amongst others but this is the one that comes out top*

It all started with a show called, "AIR CRASH INVESTIGATION"

Which I watched before even traveling on a plane. So, the first time I went on a plane I was PETRIFIED, I mean what if the plane crashed?

What if I didn't make it? Or what if someone hijacked the plane??

I had watched Neerja also by this point

Turbulence was my one enemy, and my heartbeat went down watching the plane's wings go up and down as we took a turn in the MIDDLE OF THE SKY. My favorite part of a flight to date is when it gathers speed on the runaway BEFORE taking off. Because I am one for speed, and that is another issue with planes. I cannot make out how fast we are going, and speed means only so much to me if I can't experience it.

Till date, I listen to the flight safety demonstration with perplexed concentration because,

Who knows?

I only sit in the aisle seat, so in case of an emergency, I'm quick to follow the neon strips to the nearest exit.

All this being said I still feed my fear by watching movies and shows about the same.

Cue the air hostess saying "BRACE, BRACE, BRACE" while all passengers are in fear of their, in Sully, with Tom Hanks as the captain.

Or maybe I just watch too many movies,

And pay too much attention to them, because I watched that movie just the one time in 2017 or so and I managed to by-heart a dialogue-

Anyways back to my original story

I also have the talent of telling multiple stories inside one- a story Inception if you will

Everything about the plane I saw THIS night was very pretty, soothing, and calming.

And that was a different experience in itself because these were emotions I had never related with an airplane before, it was always about the fear or how fatal this could end up being.

My line of vision followed the plane, while it flew, across all the clouds and took what seemed like an extremely swift turn, but it eventually gathered speed as the lights became fainter and it finally got lost between a cluster of red clouds.

It was one of the most beautiful things I have seen, honestly.

The main focus for me was that the people on that flight would have no idea how it all looked! How can one appreciate something if they don't know for themselves just how beautiful it really is?

All that beauty, just for me.

And it seems like such a beautiful career too.

Imagine if I decided to become a pilot one day, FACE that fear? I feel like if I can build the courage to do that, I can do anything.

The sky would be my limit *pun intended*

It's been my fantasy to be part of the cabin crew too. So, I could fly around everywhere as my job, and I mean who doesn't love air hostesses? They're so polite and hospitable that it's inspiring to me. *Again, Alia Bhatt's character, an aspiring air hostess in Badrinath Ki Dulhania played a role in helping me realize that but whatever*

The essence of that moment lies in the fact that I was so in love with the same thing I had feared for so so long

That means the world to me.

August 13th

Today was international left-handers' day.

A special day for me and people like me :)

I'm oddly proud of being left-handed even though I had no role in that aspect of my existence, per se.

It makes me feel U N I Q U E

In a way.

But also makes me feel like I fit in with the other 10% of the population

So, I stand out while fitting in, in a sense?

And that's comforting to me.

15th August

Since it was Independence Day today, I woke up early for our school's special assembly.

And my mother and I watched Shershaah today.

It was a great movie.

I'm between completing so many different projects, assessments, and speeches at the moment. I don't want school tomorrow

It's a Monday. But I'll get through because we have a long weekenddd.

It's a holiday on Friday.

ooo and I wrote a poem for the prompt 'nothing lasts forever'

" "what lasts forever? he asked.

nothing - she said

what does forever mean? she easier,

hmm, nothing - he said

so nothing is nothing?

well do you love me?

of cource I do, do you?

what does it matter,

if it means nothing...?

but or NOTHING'S means everything to me. he said. he meant it.

"everything is forever" wrote their destiny"

isn't it cute :(

and and look at the caption I came up with for this

"in a world where love is eternal

but nothing lasts forever

they didn't know who to beleive. So they just beleived one another"

It's in bold to show just how much I love it.

19th August

Rashi and I met at her place today!!! It was fun

As always.

20th August

it's 1 AM right now,

and I'm feeling outraged.

I had such a lovely day today and was in the best mood I'd been in, in months.

I got part of an outcome for something I've been working on for OVER 2 years.

Something related to it happened later on in the day.

And it made me so so sad

The impact of my happy day and all I had done towards that

just gone.

So, I decided to distract myself. I rode my cycle. After almost 2 years. I rode all my anger away at 7km/hr.

I was trying to escape my thoughts...

literally.

I ride for the speed.

I went faster and faster till that was all I could think about.

anddd the speed breaker interrupted that

just great :')

Ah, it made me feel so much better though.

When I returned, more things were added to my list of devastations...

and I just can't take it anymore. I can't sleep because

never have I ever ended a day on such a bad note.

I never go to sleep angry or upset.

Because like I've said before, on my worst days too something even subtly nice happens at the end and I count that and go to sleep.

Now I don't know what to do. I was in the balcony for a bit, but it got kind of boring so I'm back in my room. I was staring at Bangalore City, without my glasses for the first time.

Everything was so blurry, but it still felt right

I guess.

I don't know how I'm going to sleep today if I do.

22nd August

Not a single day passes that I don't miss school. Like
SCHOOL SCHOOL.
So naturally, I had to write a poem about it
The lost traveler
"get ready and tie your shoes
so tight that they can't get lose
all-day
reach the bus stop before 8:10 everyday
and school before 8:30
at 8 nine she's yelling at her schoolmates to hurry up.
the same route that they took
everyday
for years.
right turn left straight ahead.
right again and left again
and right again then left
she took the same amount of steps to reach the building
each day
and leave her bag and greet the same four faces
a prayer, pledge, news, and thought
a mistimed national anthem
but JAI HIND they said all together
3 floors upstairs with heavy bags
distribution of the newspapers
and counting the missing faces
9 classes and 2 breaks
gossip to fit through it all
dance and music and art
and football for days to come
the last bell and a walk to the bus
and then she's back home
everything calculated, same as the day before
not anymore though

not. anymore
will she ever get this back?
and if so will things be the same again
it seems,
she had lost herself between
losing this all...
but she just lost a part of herself"
and it was Raksha Bandhan today
I had loads of fun!!
26th August
Hi hi! I know it's been a while, but I just figured out the coolest thing I have in a while!!!

Remember I mentioned that flight the other day.

I saw it again today. At 10:50.

It's a Thursday and the last time I saw it was around the same time, on a Thursday too!!
I used my amazing 'stalker' skills and tracked down the flights that departed and arrived in Bangalore today *basically went to the Bangalore Airport site* but whatever.

So, I found quite a few flights but one single one landed at "22:48", today!

It was a flight of Vistara from Delhi to Bangalore.

So, I went to Google and checked the flight timings from Delhi to Bangalore for the next 3 Thursdays

And it came

This is the one!!

It may seem like a small thing but it's such a cool observation to me.

If I hadn't noticed the exact time both the times I couldn't have figured this out.

And If I didn't write about it.

Of course, I'd still remember it, but I had to come back here to see which date and day it was.

It all feels so cool.

I will look out for this flight next week too.

Somehow it just doesn't feel like a coincidence.

I mean how many people see the same flight between 2 weeks on the same day and at the same time.

While consciously realizing it.

There was something just SATISFYING about connecting all the dots

I can't put my finger to what but it's fun to write about it too.

Anyways I wanted to mention another thing about today.

So, it all started when I used to feel damn Idk lonely? In my online classes.

And I somehow ended up hating all my classes and wished I could be in the other section

When they had Geography, we had Math

So naturally, I would prefer to be there.

But when we had Geography, they had Math

And the same feeling came

Like Math over Geography???

And I ended up feeling left out even though we are all studying the same curriculum with most of the same teachers.

I'm not sure if that makes much sense but why do I always prefer being on the other side?

Even when I go out, say on a road trip

All I can think about during the journey is how amazing the destination will be and when I reach it, I'm left thinking about going back home.

Why is it?

I'm working on it though

I should try and be present in the now

pun intended

Maybe I should add a note on the cover of the book that says "all puns intended"

Oh, and a couple of days back I watched Interstellar! But I shall write more tomorrow because I'm sleepy right now.

Byee.

August 29th

I did not write in the last two days because I'd been waiting for the outcome of something amazing, over the weekend

whichh

did not happen

So, I'm not sure what I'm doing right now but hey! I guess

The thing that I wanted the outcome of was very special and something I've been very patient about. But as mad as it made me, I decided not to let it affect me, because I did my best.

I'm very self-aware you see, and sometimes that retaliates back to me. Like just now, I did my night routine (yes, I'm very sophisticated) and I was feeling like such a main character. As if someone was recording me for a movie scene as I jumped into bed, putting my blanket on as I flipped the light switch off.

My night routine is just me speaking to myself in front of the mirror for like 5 minutes before I go to sleep (shh- I don't sleep until I vent to my dairy)

This may make me sound like a crazy person, but I rather enjoy talking to myself. Ironically, it helps me maintain my mental peace. Every night, I thank the universe for everything and just talk about my day. I find that helps me categorize the emotions I felt throughout the day, and I just feel happy.

I remember watching a video that was just 30 seconds long. "How to be the main character- Casual Magic", and this lady said, and I remember exactly, "not every day is going to be your birthday, not every day is going to be the best day of your life. but does that really mean you can't find *anything* to enjoy that day?... are you going to waste the entire day?

Casual magic asks you to find something

something tiny, something small

But something beautiful. Something that stands out in the mundane every day, to be grateful for."

And it can be anything!

From the way, someone looked at you to how much you enjoyed a meal with your family.

I've been following this for the past 2 months, and I call this "highlights of my day"

I mean casual magic has a more *magical* ring to it but I had to personalize it to make it mine ;)

So, the highlights of my day today were, (I have 3 per day)

1. The call I had with my friends for an English Project (yes that's right, I made friends in my section!!)

2. Watching Dr. House with my parents

3. Staring at the rain while completing another project and listening to music

It's so simple but it just proves that everyday is not every day.

As much as I love using the word MONOTONOUS it's exactly things like this that prove my life isn't monotonous. And that gives me hope.

Speaking of main characters (I am the main character in both real life and this book hehe) today I realized that in some ways,

I am basically a compilation of all my comfort characters.

From books, movies, shows, and songs.

I was drinking lemon tea and just to make it clear before like January 2021, I drank water and only water.

Like not even exaggerating, I HATE any sort of aerated drinks (the texture of fizz on my tongue is sodjsks) and I haven't quite developed the taste for proper tea or coffee yet.

I find the fruit juice of some fruits and coconut juice *bearable* but water is the best.

See now that hasn't changed yet...

and I doubt it ever will because it has the best TASTE.

"CUE: *drumroll* haha irony."

So anyways I realized I now drank lemon tea ever so often and it's my 2nd favorite beverage.

I started drinking tea only because I wanted to accompany PATRICK JANE while he did too *I would drink it while watching The Mentalist

For whoever doesn't know Patrick Jane and Tea are like an inseparable bond *after Teresa Lisbon ofc :)*

And I didn't realize till today that even though I finished the show months back I still drink tea and it still makes me think of this.

My sarcasm and sense of humor is borrowed from Chandler Bing (F.R.I.E.N.D.S), Imraan (Zindagi Na Milegi Dobara), Cho and Rigsby (Mentalist), Michael Scott, Jim Halpert and Dwight K. Schrute (The Office), Jake Peralta (Brooklyn 99) and James Wilson (Dr. House)

All my "keen observations", psychology-related comments, and most of the scientific information I know are the simple byproduct of watching Patrick Jane, Dr. House, and Sheldon Cooper.

As for my feminine energy and self-confidence- Rachel Green, Grace Van Pelt, Amy Santiago, and of course Penny Hofstadter.

I can't even begin to mention all the teen characters I used to look up to, from KC in K.C Undercover(basically teen Znedaya) to Avery from Dog with a Blog.

Percy Jackson and Riptide, and all of the girls from Malory Towers. (Except Gwen

- wow I still remember her name)

"Gwendoline Mary Lacey, nicknamed Dear Gwendoline Mary, is one of the main antagonists of the series. She came to Malory Towers at the same time as Darrell. Gwen is vain and shallow, attaching herself to any new girl she thinks is glamorous, rich, or gifted."

-thank you Google.

no wonder I remember her and dislike her till now-

It's funny how the name of the character who I disliked is still stuck with me but I had to google the name of my then-favorite, Darell Rivers

I fantasize boarding schools to this day because of this series.

Honestly all Ruskin Bond and Roald Dahl books and of course Geronimo Stilton. Who doesn't relate to Greg Hefley in Diary of A Wimpy Kid.

Tom Hanks and Meg Ryan in You've Got Mail!!

Sunny, Kabir, Aisha, honestly everyone, and most of all, Pluto in Dil Dhadakne Do.

Rustom Pavri from Rustom.

Geet from Jab We Met and THE Phunsukh Wangdu (although everyone is like 2% Chatur) and

Shashi from English Vinglish.

JK Talpade and Atharv from The Family Man. Missy Cooper in Young Sheldon and I can't even begin to speak about the YouTubers I follow and my comfort characters in the YouTube web series.

Any Disney Princess, villain, side character, animal, or mystical creature.

I could go on and on...

All of these small fragments of which some are just ideas of people who aren't even real...

These things are perceived differently by each individual, but they make me who I am. While I always was ME, all of these characters and experiences enabled a different part that I didn't know of till then.

how cool.

now I've been writing for over 1 and a half hours-

days and days pass by with experience after experience but I don't write about it because there's "nothing to write about"

and yet I got so much from just "tea".

Yeah, I should SERIOUSLY sleep now.

Oh, and add writing today's account to my day's highlights ;)

August 30th

I just added a Grammarly extension to the document I'm writing this on and spent the last 45 minutes fixing the FOUR HUNDRED AND SEVENTEEN issues it presented me with.

Out of all those issues, about 25 or so were just "this is not a word" errors for my family and friends' names. For my name, it sends a message, "Maghna is not a word...consider changing it to Megha."

Oh, also we're near 15,000 words so I'm very excited about that. I'm just generally feeling excited. We have our project presentation tomorrow and I'm excited about that too.

Yes, it's a good day, and it's raining again.

I was supposed to complete the geography project but instead, I'm sitting with this again.

Usually, my birthday is the best time and my awaited time every year. This time I don't know if more excited about the birthday aspect or for publishing my book.

We are going to have our second set of exams in exactly 17 days, and we filled some consent forms for going back offline. Many people consented no so I'm not sure if it will re-open, most of my main-ish friends and I consented yes itself though so let's see!

I don't want Math class. All of the chapters are damn hard, and I just dislike the subject. It's ok let's just go ahead with the mindset that next year, this time that subject won't be a part of my life.

I had followed the same mentality last year with Covid. SO that backfired.

Okay, next year this time. *Touchwood*

Now I am trying to sing along to a catchy Telugu song, but I can't

Because

I don't know Telugu.

I listen to some Tamil and Malayalam songs too-

And ONE Kannada song.

English and Hindi I can sing along to. The song albums of Hindi movies these days aren't worth listening to more than once *counting the time they play during the movie*

Maybe it's my taste but most of them are just remakes of older, better songs.

So, my playlists are filled with songs of old movies, some of them I've not watched, and I wasn't even born when some were released. I don't even know where I'm going with this-

Yaa, I should probably just go and do my project.

I'll check back in after a few hours!

I'm backk, it's been 5 hours and I did one page of the project (oops). It was Krishna Janmashtami today and I had fun in the puja my mom did.

It wasn't anything special as such, but I felt nice,

I guess.

I have to study for my Chemistry test soon. I keep going back to some songs, hoping they remind me who I was when I used to listen to them.

Like, New Divide...I keep going back to it, only because it reminds me of all our annual function practices and all of my memories attached to the same. My heart keeps going back to it hoping I can have those moments of 2 years ago, again. If anything, it just makes me sadder. More aware of what I once had but don't anymore.

Right now, Gerua is playing, and I'm thinking of how Srishti and I used to yell out our lungs and sing it *all of the lyrics wrong*, almost 5 years back. Wow.

Oh yay, I hit 15,000. THIS page number is how many pages fifteen thousand words is, to anyone curious :)

I will write tomorrow about how the English activity goes, see you!

2nd September

Is it wrong to say something very very bad always happens to me whenever my days are going well for more than 2 days?

Remember the outcome thing I said a couple of days back,

Well, I got an outcome. I was so into WANTING that outcome that I didn't even consider whether it would be a good one or not.

You can guess which it was.

Anyways the last few days have been the hardest days I've had

Ever, I guess.

Ya that bad.

'Hard' days and not 'worst', because some very notable nice stuff has also happened amidst it.

Like yesterday it was Srishti's birthday, and I honestly had a lot of fun, but my day still sucked.

And our English project came out AMAZINGLY. Ma'am loved it and she laughed at all the jokes. More importantly, I enjoyed the entire process and the final show.

I couldn't let all of this nonsense affect my team.

9th September

It's been a week and I've been

well

holding up

it's not great but it's better than last week I guess.

anyways our exams are from next week and we have to start applying to colleges for 11th and 12th soon.

the dates for the first pre-boards also came

it feels like everything is happening way too fast and it all got too real too quick.

oh oh and I made a new friend!!

His name is Chaitanya and we're in the same class.

My favorite YouTuber has been uploading very regularly if that's some sort of compensation for

anything?

My current mood is to just give up on literally everything, but I should go on, I hope it's worth it.

It's like I know exactly what I wanna write and how but just

can't?

19th September

After a much-needed break of what was supposed to last just a week, I'm back.

I felt so guilty each day for not writing but I really needed that time to myself.

I have so much to write about and our exams are going on right now.

I'm gonna give a summary of the last 2 weeks since I last wrote and just well update you!

Today was actually a very nice day and it's going to be 12 in 10 minutes.

It has been raining for a while and I was trying to sleep. But the lighting keeps coming in through my window and I'm still scared of the lighting.

I'm scared of light in the dark and of dark in the light.

A friend suggested I listen to music to distract myself. Dil mere from The Local Train just got over and I'm now listening to the theme song from Bell Bottom.

I'm still scared but I'm vibing.

My rate of sacredness is directly related to how I now have to sleep alone :(

Epic Movie that was though, Bellbottom. Akshay Kumar is my favorite actor.

We have English tomorrow, and Social and Math got over on Thursday and Friday.

I will be writing briefly about all the days I missed after I finish todays :)

It wasn't an eventful day because I just watched TV for the most part and studied *barely*

I went down with Laya and Preksha at night, which was very fun. I am rather tired right now though so that's all for today!

bye.

24th September

hey :)

SO this is the summary of the 31st August through 23rd September

I do realize it's almost a month and I'll admit I got very lazy to pen it all down after reaching my halfway mark. in my defense, we had some really important exams going on as well which got over 2 days back

firstly I wrote a new poem in that time period!!

It's about my city, Bengaluru, where I've lived my entire life, and this one area I specifically like here, Jaynagar.

"picked my white shirt from the balcony

it feels warm from the sun as I want it to be

sitting in an auto

feeling the wind and the breeze

hair out of place

hair on my face

but oh, the speed

walking around for hours and hours

each few meters is a new field of vision

from shoppers to hawkers

and passers-by

you can hear the temple bells and the mosque prayers at the same time

there's a shop for every event, utility, game, and profession

Woah, and I can smell a thousand smells

roasted corn, spicy guava

or the smell of boiled peanuts on a drizzly drizzly day

South Indian eateries for days to come

a great green garden to fit all the fun

it's been a lovely day

now it's time to go home

let's all ride on the big blue bus at the prominent depot"

1ST SEPTEMBER- it was Srishti's birthday and we all had met down in the apartment and spent the evening together! I had loads of fun with her but it wasn't too great of a day overall.

2ND SEPTEMBER- me and Chaitanya chatted pretty much the entire day so that's been fun, and we had Double Geography today! *instead of Chemistry!* Speaking of friends, even Adhya and I had a fun conversation today.

3RD SEPTEMBER- we had double Chem today
what is this odd karma :')

9TH SEPTEMBER- I had written this poem on that day, as I had gone to Jaynagar

12TH SEPTEMBER- as of today I am responsible for MY happiness!!!

this has been a long term goal for so long and I'm glad I could achieve it

13TH SEPTEMBER- we didn't have school today because of some technical issues so I went down with Srishti, Preksha, Laya, and Trisha

18TH SEPTEMBER- TODAY WAS A REALLY IMPORTANT AND LOVELY DAY. PERIOD.

22ND SEPTEMBER- Trisha needed some art supplies today and since our exams got over today we all went with her to the shop on our main road. It takes around 10 minutes or so to reach and it was a great time. The same people I mentioned above had come and we all got ice cream and coke after too :)

26TH SEPTEMBER- Rashi and I went to the mall together! IT WAS A GREAT TIME. very fun

28th September
finding motivation-

judging by how I feel going back and forth with writing and little and not writing at all I guess it's obvious I'm struggling with finding the motivation to write...

Since I want this book to be as honest as I feel comfortable sharing, I will confess that I did consider dropping the entire project more than a few times.

In the mental position I was in, it seemed more like an obligation than an enjoyable pastime. At the time.

I also left a lot of space for the previous one because I have plans to fill out that a bit later.

I mean my pre-boards will start soon so I should honestly make the best of this time and just write as much as I can while I still have the time to, but it didn't feel right to do this when my heart didn't feel happy enough.

So about exams, I got an average of 74%, which may I just point out could have been 77% if I didn't consider Math marks.

Which reminds me I chose Basic Math for the boards, as I'm planning to drop it anyways.

Lately, I've been feeling extremely drained and exhausted. And just stressed. I feel sleepy enough for another night's sleep just 2 hours after waking. I'm not saying all this as an excuse as to why I didn't write but it's just worth mentioning I guess.

I don't feel like myself sometimes I guess. it's not like me to be so low and for so long too.

I read somewhere that when you feel so it can mean you're upgrading in life, which makes sense with the major energy shift.

it's a positive change I'm sure. (sure now after doubting reality for 3 days)

I was thinking about one of my favorite YouTuber's (Mridul Sharma) and how she posted 24 YouTube videos this month. It's her birthday month and she follows this ritual of posting as many videos as old as she turns every year. Whichh is a really cool concept and a big step up from the normal 8 to 9 that people usually post each month. Which is some great news for us as viewers but precisely 3 times more(yes I'm good at math when it comes to things I'm passionate about) work for the creator, be it editing, video ideas, or recording.

I found it pretty inspiring that she spends her entire birthday month doing this(and vlogs her birth day). Surely with a career like YouTube, you'd hope for a break during at least your birthday but this is really admirable.

Speaking of YouTube, it's my dream career. I want to make vlogs and share all my experiences. I love editing things and I've already filmed my first video... It's something I've shared with just close friends but the kind of video I hope to share on my channel as my very first after like 10 or so years. *full long term planning*

I'm just waiting to turn 18 so my profile doesn't come under YouTube kids, and then I will vlog my college days. And then see where it takes me

it's a pretty legitimate goal I'd say :)

Oh oh, most of the YouTubers I follow are from Mumbai. And for the longest time, my biggest dream was to watch Kapil Sharma's show live, in Mumbai. And there's this place I've heard a lot about which I wanted to go to as well, called 'Kidzania'

Since I lost interest to be an audience to his show after the recording stopped due to Covid and the age limit for going to Kidzania is 13 I lost both my reasons to visit.

This is when I realized my desire to go to Mumbai was something much more meaningful and deep. I don't know what it is yet but it feels like my true calling. It's such a pretty word.

Friends and so many other people tell me often, it's not that great, there's just pollution, you'll only like it if you've lived there, etc.

But somehow none of it even half convinces me.

When I hear people talk about the places and landmarks, the names are all so familiar in my heart somehow. It's so unexplainable but one day the dream to visit the city just entered my heart and never left. The urge just grows stronger each time I see a sky or beach picture. The rains while at marine drive or a video of the sea link. It's all so comforting.

here's a list of all the places I want to visit that no one asked for

-Mumbai

Colaba Causeway, Worli Sea Link, Marine Drive, Palladium, Nirula's, Chowpatty, Juhu, Gateway of India, Brijwasi Sweets, Churchgate, Carter Road, Taj Mahal Palace

Someday I will surely visit,

and vlog it

and upload it on my channel.

I'm coming back to write this cuz I didn't realize it at the moment. I never realize how writing is what helps me heal the most. As much as I avoided writing cuz I didn't want to face those thoughts, I will be sleeping happy today :)

8ᵗʰ October

If there's anything I learned from the last time I wrote it's that I feel better after writing so using that information to my advantage I will write this in the hope's my mood gets better.

I have a lot to tell you about yesterday but first, I have some updates on the topic of shows, I finished Dr. House and it was so so well directed. So, right now I'm re-watching The Office and Friends (i was seeing The Office side by side Dr. House anyways). I tried Seinfield for around 4 episodes but I'll continue it some other time maybe. The first episode of the new season of Young Sheldon finally came though!! So I'm really looking forward to watching that tonight

Vaise toh I don't have any 2nd update but my pre-boards are starting in 10 days. and I'm so scared. But I'll get to meet all my classmates after half a year- offline

okay so

yesterday was Sana's 16th birthday. She's been excited about this birthday for soo many months if not years. She had this big party and it was the most fun I had ever since Covid started. I met around 8 girls from school and also met all her friends. It was a great time and I was glad to see it all turned out how she wanted and she was so happy.

I took around 3 to 4-second videos every 30 minutes to compile into a mini-vlog type reel *future career reference* and the sunset was soo pretty so the end product was really pretty looking and professional ish.

She was so happy and right before we went she hugged me so tight that I felt like EVERYTHING would be alright. I have amazing friends.

10th October

There's something simply inspiring about Prateek Kuhad's songs.

because now I feel like writing.

so HI

I was attempting to study Physics but I am surprisingly great at distracting myself.

and I'm apparently going out now but I will write once I'm back *PAKKA*

12th October

okay now that we've established that the word Pakka means nothing to me let's move ahead

oh oh ya remember

like a few days *or many days* back I'd written about things I used to do but don't anymore.

I recently remembered another important thing- SOFT TOYS

So my history with soft toys is pretty old and vast.

I have a habit of collecting stuffed toys from different places, I'm practically a hoarder when it comes to most things (cutlery, stationery, you name it)

so over the years, I have a wide collection of many exotic and indigenous soft toys,

Starting with my first, a pink teddy bear the hospital gave when I was born, many different animals and characters gifted by family and friends, a pink rabbit that's the size of my palm from Pondicherry, a mouse, a baby heart, and a big heart and Humpty dumpty from IKEA, each acquired from a different trip.

and my personal favorite, an original life-size Minion from Universal Studios.

Thinking back getting Kevin *minion's name* was the SOLE reason I wanted to visit Singapore 5 years back.

such is my love for both minions and soft toys.

I still remember how I didn't trust the airport staff with him so I got him with me in the cabin luggage. He was under my seat the entire time in the bag I got when I bought him.

To be frank my level of protectiveness towards him is the same. As I write this, he is wrapped in a pink blanket from all 4 sides so his bright yellow color doesn't fade over the years.

Anyways, back to the main point, I've mentioned this before but

till I was about 14 I had to sleep with my 2 very specific soft toys.

the pink teddy bear that's as old as me and a Doraemon my parents gave me when I turned 3.

and when I 'had to' i mean that very literally, I WOULD not get any sleep if I didn't have them. It came to a point where I traveled everywhere with them. Because if not that was most definitely a sleepless night.

In addition to the places I mentioned above, two of them have traveled all over Bangalore and to Singapore too.

I felt bad about how they came this far and didn't get to see anything so I used to remove them from my bag and say "this is the bus", "this is the plane", and in the airport, in Malaysia, I gave them a whole tour!

I thought I might as well give them the entire experience you know.

I even spoke to them sometimes and they both fit perfectly side by side on my chest for me to fall asleep. I slept hugging them tightly and woke up in the same position, each day.

Hugging gave me all the comfort I needed on a bad day and all the affection on a good one. I would read them stories and ya that was just a happy part of my childhood.

And that is why it hit me so hard when one day I decided to not hold them while I sleep and I woke up the next morning with a full night's sleep.

I didn't need them anymore.

I was absolutely gutted. As a 14-year-old, I could now sleep by myself?

how...

grown up...

total Toy Story moment

they are on my bed while I sleep to this day but I will never understand how I needed them to sleep one day and didn't the next.

There are just too many things I miss about when I was younger. Some of them aren't even from memory.

Like I've seen CDs of me from when I was a baby, like anyone.

And there's this one song I really loved as a child when I was barely a year old

"where's the party tonight"

It was like my jam.

I didn't even know how to walk at the time but trust me when I tell you I used to dance to that song.

I used to go round and round banging one leg to another while sitting upright.

I didn't know I had discovered dancing before walking.

In a similar-ish way...I was seeing my scrapbook of nursey a few months back and I had been asked to paste a picture of my favorite room

15 year old me's is the kitchen.

So you can only imagine how surprised I was when I saw a kitchen's picture in there.

like yes 3-year-old Maghna you and I had some common goals

in some ways, I'm still like her

which is something that makes me happy now.

I mean when I was younger, all I ever wanted was for me to grow up

and now that I'm older I miss how I was back then

anyways back to my 3-year-old wala story

so just today I SPRINTED to my main door when my dad came back from office because I needed to open it before my mother so I could meet him first.

I used to ask my mother the question "when will he come back" at least 10 times per day and that's pretty much what I did this time too, after 2 years of having my dad set up office in the next room.

I would always run to the door like this when I was younger and excitedly hug my father before he could even enter the house.

that part I obviously don't do anymore cuz

Covid

not that anyone cares but my PC screen froze like 20 mins ago so I've been writing from my phone since.

Idk what its issue is because now it's frozen to the point where I can't switch it off.

anywhoo

I've been writing for well over an hour and I'm surprisingly exhausted so let's stop today's entry here.

goodnight, bye <3

October 16th

I am back at 12:30 of another night. Just me and my music.

I studied Computer Science today, for the first time this year I believe.

it's our first CS exam this year and JAVA is really not my thing, we have pre-boards from next week but the first exam is an internal Computer exam.

I got back to playing Guitar, this week.

and it felt really great. like Amazing.

and not to brag or anything but I really love how it sounds when I move my fingers across the strings touching each metal fret on the hardwood.

I started playing 5-6 years back and used to attend a class. We learnt many English and Hindi rhymes and songs but I left that class before I learnt Chords.

btw Alag Aasman by Anuv Jain is playing right now.

like therapy to my ears

I left mainly because I was supposed to practice playing every day for 20 minutes. My 11-year-old mind really disliked that apparently

so I left, and I didn't touch the guitar till about a month ago.

My dad had asked me to stay in touch because I had learned it and I may just forget it over the years otherwise.

at the time I only did some basic string and finger exercises.

And if anyone else is anything like me, they'd know that the outcome of something they do by their own choice is much more powerful than when they're asked to do the EXACT thing by someone else.

Because last week when I got that feeling, to play...

I played almost all the songs I'd learned

and it felt incredible.

Frankly that Inspiration to play wasn't all of my own

To me, "inspired by myself" is an oxymoron. because realizing you want to do something/ an idea about something is because of something someone said, did, or make (art/poems/videos) is all part of the process of where you get inspiration.

and you may not even realize it sometimes

but many times something big and really popular was indeed inspired by something smaller and more personal.

it's quite interesting to think about.

So anyways, my inspiration was this video I saw of an old friend.

He had told me around 2 years back that he knew how to play and I mean he was playing so very well.

I remembered that I know how to play too so why not just brush up you know actually get back to it.

maybe even learn those chords

I believe being a lefty makes playing way easier for me because with the guitar the main work is done by the left, so I feel it's better if that is your dominant hand.

oh, and that guy, he's a lefty too

another girl I know who plays really well is also a lefty.

practically all the left-handed people I know play the guitar.

maybe it's a thing idk

so anyway, today I practiced "Kal ho na ho" and tried "Piya bole".

I still need a lot of practice in "Kal ho na ho" but I really love how "Piya bole" is sounding.

since it's 1 AM now and I have to wake up at 8:30 tomorrow I will stop writing

"I nEeD tO gEt My BeAuTy SlEeP"

- said every high school character ever

18th October

We had our first UNOFFICIAL day of 10th standard today (offline) and it was alright. It was great seeing all my friends and the teachers and the school itself but not much went how I thought it would. We came to school after around 7 months and so much had changed. They had re-painted many places and added a lot of fun new cool lights etc.

The exam itself was fine, we had Computer Science today.

we stayed in the building for not more than 2 hours and most of that was the writing time, so my favorite part was when standing outside the school and talking to my friends.

There were some people who I'd been hoping to speak to but I didn't get the chance.

Now we have 2 days of study holidays for Math.

MY favorite.

Despite choosing Basic, the pre-board is going to be Standard.

I have no idea whats the logic behind that is.

and our first board dates came out today, it's starting on 30th November.

this is all getting too real.

I've been listening to 'you are in love' by Taylor Swift on loop for weeks now,

I don't think I've mentioned it yet but I'm such a big ROMANTIC.

I mean romanticizing my life is one of my strengths but I love romantic things in general.

moves, novels, songs just everything.

So I decided to whip up a nice poem for which I got the idea while listening to the song.

Enjoy my use of the poetic license and vivid imagery :)

"speaking to each to other till we hear only whispers and then fall asleep only to wake up in each other's dreams

you hold my hand tightly as we cross the road because you know I don't like doing it alone

the warmth and strong grip makes me feel we're far more powerful than the traffic on both sides

midnight kisses and teddy-bear hugs

petting kittens and spots with ladybugs

running my fingers through your hair

every curl and fluff is known to me

traveling together and eventful dinners

cozy cuddles and warm hot chocolate on rainy days with mittens

geeky intellectual conversations about our favorite shows and movies

driving around the city, near the beach or the highways
going to watch a movie and
our hands touching in the dark theater, inside the popcorn tub
we let our hand's touch in the buttery goodness
sharing playlists that make us think of each other and as I listen to yours I'm blushing myself to sleep
funny selfies and exciting voice messages
wearing each other's shirts and hoodies and buying matching rings
seeing each other's childhood photos only to realize he was this cute from the beginning
teaching each other the things we don't know in the most exciting and innovative ways
sharing a pair of earphones that is playing the common songs in both our playlists
speaking with our eyes and zoning out for seconds at a go
dissociating from reality to a world only you and I know
tagging each other in posts and spamming about one another on close friends
good night hugs and morning kisses, I can vision it from just the texts
I still sleep with the soft toy you gifted me on that summer day
jamming sessions with both our guitars
"of course I remember it all"
and the day
I told you
I love you, best friend."

I love this one soo much, I think I've already read it 5 times

27th October

hi.

I know it's been a hot minute since I last wrote but school has been SO suckish.

It's like every single day is the exact same, except for the bad parts..cuz there's a new and unexpected bad part to each day that's not the same as the previous one.

so I don't even know what to expect and that just adds to the horribleness.

I may have mentioned this already but most of my friends are in the same section, and they all speak and do everything in their exam hall together and I'm so so left out.

Chaitanya is in my class but I barely get a chance to speak to him. Not like we have any other mutual friends.

Adding to all this, I finished The Office for the second time a few days back.

and re-watching my comfort shows is practically the only thing that keeps me going.

I can't watch the others a fourth time either because I've byhearted all lines.

I'll probably just start The Office again but there isn't that much fun in watching it anymore.

I cannot for the life of me bring myself to start another. I have to re-watch...because I make up for all the unpredictability of my life by knowing exactly what's gonna happen when in which episode of which show.

I know some horrible surprise won't just come and ruin an episode.

I know it seems very shallow of me to rant on about some unimportant show or sitcom but it's just the build-up of everything that's been going on around me...

I've made some new friends, online but somehow feels like the more friends I have the more lonely I am.

that doesn't make any sense but yeah I don't know what makes sense anymore.

There's another exam left, it's English. It will take place the day after. I don't expect anything from that day anymore.

I don't think I care, I don't want to at least.

online was so much better but it's offline now and it will continue like that.

28th October

ouch, looks like I left the last one in a negative-ish tone, sorry about that.

I'm a little better today but not very?

I'm listening to "Alag Aasamaan" by Anuv Jain right now and honestly, his songs are so therapeutic to hear. and after listening to his songs after months I've finally written my first HINDI POEM!!

to be honest I feel like a songwriter at this point than a poet but that's cool too ;)

part of me wants to compose this into an actual song because I find the lyrics beautiful. *then I can be the next Olivia Rodrigo* just kidding ik it's not that nice also.

anyways let me add it

"ek baar dekh le

jab hum rehtain hai ghoorte

aur duniya main kuch dikhta hi nahi

hum kuch aur sochtain bhi nahi

aur

har baar. 'vo' hai toot jatha, kisi aur ki vajah se …

mujhe ghar nahi jaana

naahi hai tujhe

ah..arrey

tum chale gaye...

ek baar mujhe dekha bhi nahi..mudke

tu.chala.gaya
main reh gayi yahan par,
har kahin tumhari yaadon ki dhoond main
har cheez main, har jagah pe, har chehre par
tumse bohot door,
main ab bhi hoon khadi yahan...
apni gali main
baar baar mudti reh gayi
teri dhoond main."
ironic that I'm sitting and writing poems in Hindi a day before my English exam.

I had watched Sardar Udham with my mom just a few days back and I was so happy to know that it may get nominated for an Oscar. I mean the movie was really amazing and it showed every event as it truly happened, it had no songs, no extra characters just the raw description of the events, which is something that everyone should know. and Vicki Kaushal's extraordinary acting.

and then I saw this headline today

"Indian jury rejected Sardar Udham as India's entry for Oscars: 'it projects hatred towards British'"

I was so upset when I saw this but I mean what's the point of a Biopic if the events aren't shown AS THEY HAPPENED? it should honestly be appreciated that a movie was made showing the truth.

I mean mine is a very subjective opinion but this news upset me a lot for some reason

anyways ill go study for a bit

byee

3rd November

'oh "dear diary" I met a boy'

what a cheesy way to start an entry na?

Except I was just singing a song. I'm always singing pretty much, and weirdly enough many times the songs that I'm singing aren't even ones I like. It's just odd and catchy but they're stuck in my head 24/7.

Anyways,

Yesterday was the first day of SCHOOL

After well over a year, *we have only gone to write exams till now* we had a proper 5 hour school day and except for how long and exhausting it was, my day sucked pretty much. As I've made more than clear I do not have many friends in this section so I was alone for the most part, lonely rather.

So I went to school in that vibe today too

and WHAT A DAY IT WAS

It was a big step up and ya I'm just happy

mental note to self- Second days are alwayssss better than the first days

I'm saying that because in my case at least I have exceptionally high expectations of first anything's, in my case, the first day of offline school. When everything I'd thought about school was not even half as good as I wanted is it to be, yesterday...

I went in today, prepared for a bad day

Expectation is key I guess. When it's there something always goes wrong but when there is no expectation everything will always turn out better

I mean today's Hindi class was the best.

and we got all our marks.

DESPITE doing pretty well in everything my average is 73% again and I'm pissed.

I mean Math is always bringing everything down, cuz I had to write the standard Math paper for pre-boards despite choosing basic.

I got 36 on 40 in English and I was soo happy!

I AM happy rather.

The main exams start on the 30th of this month and it's Diwali tomorrow.

And thinking back as much as I very desperately miss all my friends and classmates my class isn't all that bad

I'm beginning to like some of them.

You know how when people are reading books and they are reading this one quote, a single conversation and think that DAMN.

That makes so much sense.

And it could be something that really makes you think and changes your perspective even.

For me, it's that kind of thing that stays with me for so so long and even starts to show in everything I do and everywhere I go.

Such is the effect I want my poetry to have on people someday.

ON A TOTALLY UNRELATED NOTE *NOT*

I wrote a new one today and it may or may not be related to what happened in school, its the shortest one I've written till date but probably the cutest too.

"The things that I would do
to relive that moment with you
it happened out of the blue
everything just fell in place
and my heart a steady pace
for I could see it on your face
you missed me too
man,
you. missed me. too."

Judging by how I started writing poems just 11 months ago, last December, I love the improvement I'm making in terms of using better words, rhyme scheme, poetic license, imagery, and such.

What if when I look back I can see an improvement from what is my first entry in this book compared to that last one.

10th November

EXACTLY a week after my best day in months I am back on one of my mellower-saddish days. FUN FACT: I didn't know till today that mellow did not mean 'down' or sad.

It's supposed to be a positive emotion??

anyways I'll continue to use it in such context,

I usually don't write when I'm in such a mood because honestly, that's not good content but let's just give it a shot. Tomorrow's the 11th of November and as someone who's an avid believer of Angel numbers. 11:11 being the luckiest of all I expect tomorrow will be somewhat better.

I scored 74.5% in my pre-boards in REALITY cuz the calculation was *Math* I had calculated it wrong earlier.

A 1.5% increase is still an improvement so I'm still happy.

OH OH you know our seniors have been having their Practicals for pre-board, which typically means doing stuff in the Chemistry or Physics lab wearing those really cool white lab coats *which we haven't had an opportunity to wear yet because we haven't even done a single thing like that because of COVID*

So anyways the practicals include Psychology and yesterday between Math, me and 8 other people were called to the 12th grader's exam hall and we all sat with one person each. And we had to go do some tests in a specific amount of time and then our seniors were supposed to grade us and calculate how we did. It was some intelligence test type of thing and it had 60 questions, divided into 6 sets with 10 questions each, and I had 4 minutes for every 10 questions.

Most of them were to do with English or just General Knowledge. But one set was of patterns, of numbers. OF MATH. I couldn't even finish that one on time.

Anyways this was something I'm very interested in and I can totally see myself testing someone like this after 2 years.

it was so cool.

and I got to know today that I scored 94%

that's soo cool.

It's Rashi's birthday in 4 days

and I'm soo excited!!

most of my friends birthdays come in October-November only

Just last week was Navya's birthday and we had met. We're meeting for Rashi's birthday too!

Somehow offline school is also slowly becoming monotonous.

YES I'M BACK WITH THAT WORD. LET'S COPYRIGHT IT FOR ME.

Anyways from the 18th of this month, we have study holidays till the board exam so it's not too long you know.

The first exam is on the 22nd but it's Sanskrit..so myy first one is on the 30th.

even though it's just 10:30 I am oddly exhausted from school so ill try and sleep.

GUNIGHT <3

18 November

The study holidays for the exams started todayyy.

in this past week, I've had the birthdays of 3 friends. which is a lot of meetups!

Rashi and Adhya share a birthday but both their parties were on different days.

BOTH the meet-ups were really fun and Sakshi's birthday was just yesterday! We're going to be meeting tomorrow for that.

Although it's been just 8 days since I last wrote, believe it or not, I wrote THREE or more poems in that time frame.

I can't vouch for how good they are if they are but I'm loving the consistency.

To be very frank in a non-braggy way I love the poems I write

a lot!

I especially love coming back and reading and reliving the thoughts and stuff that was going on in my head when I had written an old piece. SOMEHOW capturing and capsuling those thoughts to store forever is very important to me.

to be able to feel a thing you felt in a certain way,

its an experience.

So a few days I'd written about myself, and my personality. It was a hard one to frame because I had to obviously face the truth myself before anything.

And I usually get around 50 likes on every poem I post (which is not a lot by any means but again I do it for myself)

This poem. THIS one that I especially love, has a very different style to what I usually write, so I was pretty nervous to post it.

It's rather deep and makes you question little things so I thought that would be interesting as well.

I mean I get that that's not too enjoyable for someone who just reads for fun but anyways

I barely got any comments and only around 30 likes...

which is definitely extremely demotivating.

SO this is the kind of stuff that pushes me to keep most of my work private.

Some of which I'm not even open to adding on here,

just because.

Here's this one :)
"AT THE LOST AND FOUND
hi, dear...
you can find the abandoned personality's on the left, the half-completed hobbies on the right, the confused mindsets are wandering all over the place(what a nuisance)
and that big section over in the middle is the vacancy of each soul. These are the ones that didn't find THEMSELVES after a specific event for most, that's why it's the biggest. No one ever comes looking for them.
which of these are you looking for?
hello...
I parted with a part of myself a couple of years back
just looking to take her back I guess
oh!
who is she?
oh, she's everything.
my little ball of joy. my positivity and that sparkle in my eye. the ability to not care what others think. she makes my friends laugh and does her own thing
she's my little island of personality.
I thought I'd lost her all this while
but alas!
I remembered at the right time
now that I'm back to get her
it seems like this was a safe space to keep her
while I was busy with my life.
not so much 'lost'
as unavailable to feel
I've been through so much but it's getting better now
I tried.
I tried
to get you back

I missed you so much
like a favorite toy I always had...
it's safe for your return now, let's go. I'm sorry I'd lost you but
I'm so glad you're back
"you can't lose your personality silly, she was just hiding till it was safe to come back out"
her soul whispered while a comfortable feeling overcame her"
I don't know how well I got across what I had in mind but the first few lines are like THAT lady who sits at the desk of any normal office, thus indicating the idea that your soul/ a part of you is in a safe place like this when you are going through a rough patch,
And the personality island is an Inside Out reference!
because it's those few things that make you YOU
anyways regardless of everything I love that I could come up with something of such deep meaning.
Where I live, its been raining for over a week now?
on and off but on mostly,
It's so wet and dirty all the time. Even as I'm writing this it's been raining since almost 8 AM continuously. It's 10 PM right now.
And I have this friend, who very passionately dislikes the rain,
let's call her, that friend 'Scoobster' ;)
So I kept seeing her stories and all and getting subconsciously inspired till I wrote a RAINY DAY POEM!!!
I have nothing against the rain as such, but I just dislike it.
it's just sad
IDK why

It makes me feel a Lil lonely, cold and wet, and just not nice?
anyways here is the piece,
"every time it rains
my heart thinks of you
there isn't enough water in this downpour
to fill that void you made
in the now dry seasonal river that my heart is
as much as it hurts it gives me comfort too...
with every drop that falls on the wet earth, I feel a little lost but found too
connected to the nature
but detached too
at least we share the same clouds.., some
I wonder if you feel the pain
that I do
when you see the rain too.
so many love rain
but I know you despise it too
the cold cold weather makes my heart feel cold too
when I think how we are supposed to be sharing a blanket together,
or making hot coco
wearing each other's hoodie's
or simply dancing in the rain.
there's so much I want to do
but where are you...
so I sit, up on a ledge
with my sole soul
and listen to
"baarishein"
as I close my eyes to in hope that when I wake it's not raining

anymore"

and the last one I wrote today which is proper PRIVATE only

I had started some sample papers for Social Science almost an hour ago. I attempted around 15 questions and I've been listening to music and just writing since then.

OH and remember I'd been wanting to meet someone for quite a few days,

in school

well today was the last day and I did not say hi

BIG OOPS

I've decided that it's fine.

I can try again next month, I guess...

but I've become "mature" in the sense that I'm not being sad about it,

TRYING REAL HARD NOT TO BE SAD

at least

The effort is what counts. I shouldn't be so hard on myself :)

"I can't help falling in love with you" right now. It's the version that plays in Crazy Rich Asians

I have more than 10 days of study holidays so I'm gonna ask you to wait like 4 days before I say this is also being monotonous.

Ya, I should get back to Social now,

Buh bye!

23rd November

You ever heard the term

"made my day"

it would make my day to know that I made someone else's day.

I later learned that you can not only make someone's day

but someone's week, month, or in certain cases even their year

I would be so honored to do any of that, but I can only imagine the amount of happiness I'd feel if someone made my day.

but what if I told you

as a human being

you had the power to

and are you ready for this?

make someone's existence.

you gave their life a new meaning.

maybe you told them something that won't leave their mind for a minute of a day for the rest of their lives.

or rather.

that thought

will make its home up in your head.

for how often can it go back and forth cuz u remember it too often.

that's such an awesome power to hold, as an individual

and it's just such a beautiful cycle to follow.

it sounds rather far-fetched, I know..' make someone's existence'

Telling someone something their ears have yearned to hear. That truth from your mouth after so many years.

Finding someone like yourself and souls connecting ever so effortlessly.

Or maybe,

just maybe

even something as basic as an

"are u okay.."

when the whole world is too busy with their problems.

their work

u feel very invisible?

like u don't matter
ok I've hit rock bottom.
my life seems meaningless
I have no friends
I haven't been okay
days have become months
no one even noticed.
no one seems to care
they wouldn't understand anyways..
and that's when it comes when you least expect it,
knocking on your door.
"are u okay? man! you've seemed off for a couple months"
she worries about me?
she cares about me?
she noticed?
she understands?
she asked?
she asked.
"ma'am, u just made my existence"
I was in a very writer-y mood today hence the
I don't know what this is called.
or if writer-y is a word.
Nevertheless, I'm in a brilliant mood today.

T'was a pretty normal day so it's a sudden wave of happiness that has overcome me. Not that I'm complaining though.

I've noticed I use better words and a wider vocabulary when I'm happier, versus how I normally write. *which is at best 5th-grade level*

I'm listening to a Hindi dance songs playlist and I'm bouncing up and down while dancing in my seat. Fact being that my 16th birthday is in almost exactly 2 months and I still behave like a child.

damn, this book would have been released by then.
"she's small, timid, so new
new to the ways of the world.
I want to save her,
keep her protected for as long as possible
she wants to see the world
I wish we'd spoken for longer
well, I guess she knows what she's doing
where are you from I asked
"I am from ABOVE"
she said just that much
and went her way
what did she mean by "above"
um god...
is that you
who is she?
The kitten from the 14th floor
She said no to the help,
I wanted to get her home
But she wanted to stay outside
So I just left her some milk
Morning came,
she's gone,
the milk container is licked clean :)"

SO there was this family of a cat and its kittens on the floor above mine, which is a really high floor and they all lived in the utility. No one lives in that house so I don't even know how they all came there, but anyways a few days back we stopped hearing them. So today I met a small kitten on the stairs of my floor and she was soo terrified but my God so cute. We meow-ed to each other for so long that it felt like we actually spoke. *I can meow pretty well and many times the cats also respond to me which is honestly really adorable*. And when I tried to go near her she got more scared and went down a couple of steps. So I let her be and came back but my mom left her some milk. I hadn't thought she would drink it honestly, because the bowl was a bit far from her but in the morning the container was empty and the kitty was gone :(

24th November

GUYS

KITTY HAS RETURNED.

SHE DRANK THE MILK THIS EVENING TOO.

I was just thinking about how around this time every year we have our Annual Day in school.

This would have been my last in this school.

of all the years I've been in my school, since nursery, I can't remember a year when I was not a part of the annual day, and the interesting thing is I've participated in everything at some point or another...majorly dance, sometimes music, in theatre and even in the backstage work for props and stuff.

It is uncanny that my 8th-grade annual day was my last one.

I wouldn't have believed it if someone had told me this back then. Same thing with the field trip, ah I'm so nostalgic and sad right now.

The Annual Day has always been one of the or rather the only highlight event in a school year. We start to practice months and months in advance and spend so much time perfecting every step and going over every choreography so many times.

The starting of November is always the best time. The practices last the entire day, so we are never in the classrooms. And that is also the time when we start practicing at the auditorium, than at school. It's right across the road but it is such a grand building, The best part is when the other groups and grades are practicing their bit we get to just sit in the audience and watch them. Chatting with our friends, chilling in the AC, it's all just so much fun.

WAS so much fun rather...

Ah, anyways..by the end of it everyone knew everyone else's choreography too, by watching them do it so many times.

Sometimes I feel like if I don't write all this down while I still remember it ill just forget it, forever. And it'll be like it never happened.

That thought haunts me.

That's why I want to pen down the entire world and more.

I will write until I have my words

I will write till my heart has ink no more.

damn that got poetic

anyways as i was saying

The main day when we performed was always rather bittersweet. Of course, we'd wanna give our parents a great show and let our and our teacher's efforts shine. but at the time same we didn't want all the fun to end.

We would report to school early in the morning, for a show that began after 6 PM

The teachers would spend hours fussing over our makeup, fixing every button, and making sure we look perfect. Then we would get these 'snack boxes'..with, I think, one sandwich or bun, one juice(usually mango-flavored tetra packs), chips, and something sweet.

It so happened that we were given these snack boxes AFTER we had just perfected our looks.

What a sight it was to see people eat and drink while trying not to smudge their lipsticks.

After eating we'd fix each other's makeup again and apply so much more blush and whatnot, even to the boys.

They would always wipe it off as soon as we put it and we'd just apply it again. This happened almost 2-3 times till the teacher said "DONT REMOVE THAT"

Sometimes the teacher would apply the lipstick to the guys too. And more often than not it was some common lipstick that was applied to around 20 children. THAT I don't miss.

I can still feel the nerves I always felt the moment RIGHT before we went on the stage.

As nervous as I was, the performance got over all too soon each time.

The thoughts that went through my head while performing- "OKAY keep smiling, keep smiling, don't mess up the steps, do it on the right count, have fun, okayy so where are my parents *proceeds to scan the auditorium* ok shoot I found them, um I'm more nervous now they're looking right at me, ok ok look away. Phew this is the final step and POSEEE smile andd walk off the stage"

We were all so POINTLESSLY happy right after we performed. The vibes were so happy, we were so hyper and loud.

It was night by the time everything was done and let me tell you, the vibes of a school at night are SOMETHING ELSE.

This was the only night in a year that we could experience being in school at night and we would soak it all up.

thinking back I wish I had soaked some more knowing it was the last but it's fine.

There was so much chaos at the gate when we had to go home. So many happy parents, "WE LOVED IT!" "YOU GUYS WERE SO GREAT"
Teachings trying to ferry kids out of the school so they can go home too and the very RUSH outside the gate.
I'd always feel an odd vacancy..at this point
because something we had worked so hard for, for so long
The most valued and cherished event of that year
was just over.
I'd think "well there's always next year :)"
well....
is there?

SO that was the annual day.
I think today's account is also written pretty bittersweetly itself.
That's how I'm feeling..right this moment
is more bitter than sweet,
rather
it's all bitter.
IT SEEMS LIKE I'M TALKING ABOUT DARK CHOCOLATE LMAO
Well, me and my humor defense mechanism.
it is a good joke though.

right now it isss 11:21PM

And you know 10th grade is when we got to be in charge of all the cool stuff too.

VICE CAPTAINS, SCHOOL MAGAZINE EDITORS, SCHOOL ASSEMBLY ORGANISERS

Not that I'd qualify for any of those but we are missing out on some pretty cool stuff here.

Everyone is missing out on cool stuff...

every single person

because of this pandemic

its all different stuff, of different importance to every person

Wow big picture stuff

Anyways

I just hope we can have our farewell

29th November

My exams start tomorrow

and I am petrified.

so nervous.

2nd December

HAPPY DECEMBER!!!!

It's the last month of the year

wow.

I Really missed writing the past few days but thinking back it was only because I knew I didn't possibly have the time to.

Cuz now that I do I'm not quite sure what to write about.

So 2 of my Board Exams are done.

We had Science today and the Social day before,

they were eh pretty average..better than I expected not gonna lie but I'm just happy it's over now.

We have Math the day after and I'm not freaking out for once guess why? ;)

I'm very distracted this very minute because I keep closing the tab where I'm writing this to sing along to the lyrics of the songs I'm listening to.

so let me pause it while I tell you everything about the exams

okay it's been a couple of hours, I'll tell you about school in a minute but

putting that on hold for some time...

I guess it was a good day only

ya ok that's a stretch

let's just say not a bad day.

3rd December

'3rd of December, me in your sweater'

That song is stuck in my head today

Obviously because of the date

So about the exam

I was very distracted and tired yesterday so I'm gonna tell you all about it today!

SO since the exams are happening in 'winter' it starts at 11:30

And we have to come to school by 10 or so for that

So when I came to school we first had to keep our bags in a room and they checked our pockets and stuff.

Then we just sat there with the full grade till 10:30, and then went to our exam halls.

WHICH

interesting story

Remember how they shuffled our classes?

So they've made our exam seating arrangement the same as that classes.

So I'm with 10 other people from my original '8A' section as luck has it,

Rashi, Navya, and Sana are all together

in the same exam hall...like even though each hall was allowed just 11 people they all ended up together

which is pretty nice for them but I mean

I'm pretty alone again

how does that even end up happening

Adhyaa and Ayaan are there though but they have their own friends in the same class too so we don't really talk.

Heer is with me, and we have been speaking quite a lot as she is with me in the current 10th section too.

So I was happy about that.

I was REALLY nervous before the exam. I mean my first board exam and IDK I'm just generally nervous before exams. And I was on the first bench. I was looking around at everyone before the teacher distributed the papers and I looked over at Heer who was also on the first bench, but on the opposite side. She was looking at me too and smiling while giving a best of luck sign.

I felt really warm at that moment and that really calmed me down for the paper.

The time passed surprisingly quickly and I took 30 minutes just to color the OMR sheet, which is a pretty fun thing to do not gonna lie.

So yes I guess that's about it!

7th December

We had 4 study holidays for Hindi and 2 for English.

We had one day each for Science, Social, and MATH but 4 days for Hindi

nice.

So Hindi is the day after and English is on the 11th

After that we're donee.

Did I tell you how Math went?

so mine was basic right. It was the easiest Math exam I've written in quite some time. I mean I did make a few mistakes but almost one-third of the paper was mental Math! (see now I'm using fractions and all)

9th and 10th December

It's going to be 12 in 2 minutes so I can take this as 10th December too.

We had our Hindi exam today which was a little tough but ive done well.

As a DAY, today sucked a lot, to be honest.

I'd made some big plans for school and none of it worked out. even slightly.

and it's the same thing I've been trying to do since 2 months!!

it shouldn't have to be this hard.

and whatever I am doing is just not

working.

I don't know

It's 00:00

military time.

lights are off, except for the light from my PC. Taylor Swift songs are all playing and in the queue.

I'm feeling like a mood this fine night. (MID-night)

why is it called MID night though

is it really the MIDDLE per se?

Shouldn't 3 AM or something be in the middle?

I don't know if I'm making sense right now.

oh and this is officially 100 pages :)

I'd tried blackout poetry yesterday

which was pretty cool

blackout poetry is basically a form of 'found' poetry, meaning that you select the words that catch your interest from another text making sure they make sense and can design a new poem. After you're done with that, usually with a black marker, color over the words you won't need.

SO I took a random page from a book I don't read anymore and this is what I came up with from that page.

I'm not too sure if it makes a lot of sense too

but

" used to look at the moon for hours,

felt a strange sensation in my heart

a loving home

always "

12th December

So I announced this book yesterday!!!

and the response I got was very overwhelming.

I just hope these many people read it too

it all feels very real suddenly.

14th December

Had the worst day in a while.

I've been trying to say hi to that friend for over 2 months at this point but I don't think I can,

and I keep trying not to write about so I only write when I finally get to say that YES. I did it.

I don't understand most of this anymore.

exams are over,

I still have absolutely no work to do

it's been almost 6 months with these sections and I'm anything but used to it.

I'd switch to my original section in a heartbeat.

and soon enough another unimportant exam will come and pass and the cycle goes on and on.

man this is really starting to get to me.

me.

m e

ME

such a short word
but it means so much
I mean the title is 'this is me'.
but
Who am i really?
I mean
You know how every book and most movies have that one moment when the main character turns their life around.
Like their life is a pile of monotonous and seemingly unimportant, inconsequential stuff
and then in the last few pages, there's always
a moment of realization
of how they wanna turn their life around
and how they find their true joy in seeking that
Does that really happen in real life? I mean the whole point of me writing a book was for it to be relatable on a universal scale.
Don't get me wrong, there's nothing I enjoy more than reading such books and imagining such lives
but is it very realistic?
Say to maybe ME and anyone reading this
And if so am I writing about the ME before or after this big glow-up or realization
ya, I'm not really sure if I'm making sense right now.
What if I'm still looking for 'her' by the end of this book
and what if i don't
find her...
Is that really the fairytale ending the Maghna who STARTED this book would have wanted?
Or is that the final character development waiting to happen
you tell me.

~ and she lived monotonously ever after ~

Epilogue

You know a good friend of mine had told me to write the last one on a good day

leave a bit of positivity and maybe the outcome of THE incident that I have been waiting for

all along pretty much

but you know

it's not happened yet

I don't know if it ever will

I FEEL it will,

sometime.

But whatever happens, will be for the best

so let's just leave things like that

this whole experience was something so different and cool and -

In a world that seemingly always let me down

It was truly empowering for me to CREATE my own happiness.

- okay last pun :)

I am sad tonight.

but this.

THIS

it makes me so happy

so joyful.

and as for how I wanted the word count to be over 30,000

maybe that's something we can achieve another time

I can't believe it took me so many months to understand it's not the quantity but the quality that matters.

I mean it is a common quote which I didn't even find great but to understand it from experience has made the meaning much greater and one I'll never forget

While I had the power to give myself the best of endings. Maybe even THE fairytale happy ending I've always dreamt of, maybe even waiting on wrapping up the book till I finally have a good day and share the outcome.

I chose to leave it on a pretty ambiguous note...I don't know why I did that. Maybe it's something more realistic?

All that being said. It's all good because

HER story didn't end on the last page as much as it started on the first.